Intensive Care and Clinical Biochemistry

Teach thy tongue to say 'I do not know'
and thou shalt progress.

from frontispiece to 'Retrolental Fibroplasia a Modern Parable' by W.A. Silverman

CLINICAL BIOCHEMISTRY IN MEDICINE

Series Editors: Danielle B Freedman MB, BS, MRCPath
William Marshall MA, PhD, FRCP, FRCPath
Gwyn McCreanor BSc, PhD, MRCPath

ROTHERHAM PUBLIC LIBRARIES

Intensive Care and Clinical Biochemistry

PETER GOSLING, BSc, PhD, FRCPath, ABSM

Principal Clinical Biochemist, Department of Clinical Biochemistry at Selly Oak Hospital Birmingham, Honorary Research Fellow, University of Birmingham.

WILLIAM J MARSHALL, MA, PhD, FRCP, FRCPath

Senior Lecturer in Clinical Biochemistry, King's College School of Medicine and Dentistry, University of London.

MICHAEL C CLAPHAM, MB, BS, LRCP, MRCS, FRCA

Director of Intensive Care and Consultant Anaesthetist, Solihull Hospital, West Midlands.

ACB VENTURE PUBLICATIONS

with generous support from AVL Medical Instruments UK Ltd., Instrumentation Laboratory UK Ltd. and Radiometer Ltd.

ACB VENTURE PUBLICATIONS

Chairman and Managing Editor — David Burnett.
Business Manager - Roy Sherwood

CLINICAL BIOCHEMISTRY IN MEDICINE

Series Editors — Danielle B Freedman , William J Marshall and Gwyn McCreanor.

British Library Cataloguing in Publication Data.

A catalogue record for the book is available from the British Library.

ISBN 0 902429 06 X ACB Venture Publications

Design and Illustration — Michael Cartwright and Robert Bushell

Printed by Piggott Printers (Cambridge) Ltd.

Preface

Those clinical biochemists who venture on to the intensive care unit enter a clinical specialty which is exciting, highly specialised and which can be frighteningly unfamiliar. This book is an attempt to explain, in a form which we hope will be accessible to both medical and non-medical readers, relevant aspects of the care of patients in intensive care which will place the role of the laboratory and the clinical biochemist in context.

Much benefit can arise from close collaboration between the laboratory and the intensive care unit. Such a collaboration can lead to an appropriate and cost effective delivery of biochemistry services, provide an environment which fosters research and is never boring ! If this contribution to the ACB Clinical Biochemistry in Medicine series encourages the reader to leave the laboratory to work more closely with those caring for the critically ill and review the laboratory services to the ITU, then it will have been worthwhile.

The authors wish to acknowledge the patience of Gwyn Mc Creanor, Danielle Freedman and David Burnett in nursing the manuscript from first drafts to the final stage of production. Any errors or oversights are entirely the responsibility of the authors.

November 1994
PG, WJM and MCC

ACKNOWLEDGEMENTS

The Authors are grateful to the following for permission to reproduce or adapt material for certain figures used in this publication:

Gower Medical Publishing, London. Illustrated Textbook of Clinical Chemistry, William J. Marshall (1992) (Figures 3.1 and 3.2)

CONTENTS

ABBREVIATIONS USED

ARDS	Adult respiratory distress syndrome
CAVHD	Continuous arteriovenous haemodiafiltration
CAVH	Continuous arteriovenous haemofiltration
CaO_2	Arterial blood oxygen content
CMV	Controlled mandatory ventilation
CcO_2	End capillary oxygen content
CO	Cardiac output
CPAP	Continuous positive airway pressure
CvO_2	Mixed venous oxygen content
CVP	Central venous pressure
DBP	Diastolic blood pressure
DIC	Disseminated intravascular coagulation
DO_2	Oxygen delivery
ECMO	Extracorporeal membrane oxygenation
EDV	End diastolic volume
ESV	End systolic volume
FiO_2	Fraction of inspired oxygen
Hb	Haemoglobin
HbO_2	Oxyhaemoglobin
HFJV	High frequency jet ventilation
HR	Heart rate
ICP	Intracranial pressure
IHD	Intermittent haemodialysis
IMV	Intermittent mandatory ventilation
INPV	Intermittent negative pressure ventilation
IPPV	Intermittent positive pressure ventilation
MAP	Mean arterial pressure

MPAP	Mean pulmonary arterial pressure
ODC	Oxygen dissociation curve
$P50$	50% Hb saturation with oxygen
$P95$	95% Hb saturation with oxygen
$P_{A}CO_2$	Alveolar carbon dioxide - partial pressure of alveolar carbon dioxide
$PaCO_2$	Arterial carbon dioxide tension
$P_{A}O_2$	Alveolar oxygen - partial pressure of alveolar oxygen
PaO_2	Arterial oxygen tension
PAOP	Pulmonary artery occlusion pressure (or wedge pressure)
PB	Barometric pressure
PEEP	Positive end expiratory pressure
PH_2O	Water vapour pressure
PSV	Pressure support ventilation
PvO_2	Venous oxygen tension
PVR	Pulmonary vascular resistance
RQ	Respiratory quotient
SaO_2	Arterial oxygen saturation
ScO_2	End capillary oxygen saturation
sf	Shunt fraction
SIAD	Syndrome of inappropriate antidiuresis
SpO_2	Pulse oximeter saturation
SO_2	Oxyhaemoglobin saturation %
SV	Stroke volume
SvO_2	Mixed venous oxygen saturation
SVR	Systemic vascular resistance
TPN	Total parenteral nutrition
VO_2	Oxygen consumption

Chapter 1

Shock

INTRODUCTION

Intensive care medicine, also known as critical care medicine, originated as a result of the development during the 1950s of intermittent positive pressure ventilation for the management of patients with respiratory failure. Respiratory care units were established where such patients could be treated and were the forerunners of today's intensive therapy units. Advances in cardiac surgery in the 1960s, necessitating the provision of intensive postoperative nursing care, provided another stimulus for the development of intensive care medicine, and the latter has itself been a factor which has helped to make possible the dramatic advances in surgery that have taken place in recent years.

Although the need for ventilatory support remains the most frequent cause for admission to most ITUs, the scope of intensive care medicine has expanded to include the management of a wide variety of patients with medical and surgical disorders. Critically ill patients with cardiovascular or respiratory disturbances may have actual or impending failure of other vital organs leading to multiple organ failure, which represents a major challenge in critical care medicine. The term 'intensive therapy unit' is often preferred to 'intensive care unit', and this emphasises the active nature of patient management. Individual patient care by skilled specialist nurses, continuous monitoring of physiological parameters such as heart rate, systolic blood pressure, central venous pressure, electrocardiography, etc., facilitates the early detection of any change in the patient's condition. Other parameters, including the concentration of plasma constituents can only be determined intermittently at present. Careful monitoring of fluid input and output, and drug administration together with the patient's response to them, is vital, as is the immediate availability of specialist medical personnel, allowing rapid therapeutic decision making. Thus co-ordination of the various disciplines serving the ITU is essential for maximising patient care.

From the perspective of clinical biochemistry, both clinical biochemist and physician require an understanding of the nature and means of detection of physiological and biochemical derangements that occur in the critically ill. The clinical biochemist's role should not only be the provision of timely and reliable data, but also the provision of informed advice concerning the selection, performance and interpretation of biochemical investigations.

Understanding biochemical changes in critically ill patients demands a practical understanding of the underlying pathophysiological mechanisms. Initially this may appear an impossible task for the clinical biochemist given the wide range of conditions which may lead to a patient being admitted to the ITU. Whatever the initiating process may be, a common pathway leading to cellular dysfunction, failure and cell death can be discerned. Patients reaching the ITU are by definition those who have failed, or are likely to fail to respond adequately to treatment, putting them at risk of widespread cellular failure or 'shock', organ failure and ultimately death. Fundamental to the management of critically ill patients is the avoidance of shock associated with widespread cellular failure.

Accordingly the authors have approached the understanding of the biochemical changes in the critically ill, and the basis for therapy, in terms of the pathophysiology of shock at the cellular level, the vital organs and finally in terms of the whole patient.

DEFINITION OF SHOCK

Over 100 types of shock have been described ranging from aerial shock, bomb shock, burn shock, delayed shock, electric shock, hypertensive shock, intestinal shock, to septic shock and even railway shock. At first sight it is not apparent that there is any common aspect to these conditions. The term shock was first used in 1740 by John Sparrow who translated Le Dran's 'Treatise of reflections drawn from experiences with gunshot wounds' (1731). The history of the understanding of shock is intimately associated with the history of wounds, especially war wounds. The reduction in mortality from war wounds from over 70% in the Trojan wars as described by Homer in the Iliad to 13% in the Vietnam war is largely due to the better understanding and treatment of shock. In 1826 Travers described shock as 'A species of functional concussion by which the influence of the brain over the organ of circulation is deranged or suspended'. The importance of circulatory failure in shock was further recognised by Crile in 1899 who described low blood pressure in experimental animals. By the 1940s wound shock was described as 'The clinical manifestation of an inadequate volume of circulating blood accompanied by physiological adjustments of the organism to a progressive discrepancy between the capacity of the arterial tree and the volume of blood available to fill it'.

As techniques for the restoration of blood volume following injury became more effective, it became clear that some patients (albeit fewer) still suffered 'shock', despite restoration of normal haemodynamics. These observations lead to the concept that shock may be due to structural and metabolic changes brought about in the cells that make them fail to function. This encompasses failure of the supply of essential nutrients to the cell and removal of metabolites from the cell. These changes may be secondary to poor perfusion as in hypovolaemic or cardiogenic shock, or due to some toxic agent as in septic shock or poisoning. It is hard to differentiate between cellular failure due to a toxic agent which leads subsequently to microcirculatory failure, and failure of the microcirculation and cellular perfusion, leading to cellular failure. In either event there is a stage of reversible cellular failure, through which all patients pass other than those destroyed instantly, which has been called shock or the 'reversible stage of dying'. Thus for the purposes of understanding biochemical changes in the critically ill shock can be defined as:

'Any event which leads to a significant interruption of both the supply of essential nutrients to the cells, and the removal of metabolites from the cell'.

Cellular nutrients in approximate order of priority are oxygen, glucose, water, electrolytes, nitrogen, lipids, vitamins and trace elements. The role of the intensive care unit at its most basic, can be considered as the maintenance of cellular function, by supporting the supply of essential nutrients to the cell and the removal of metabolites, in the critically ill.

CELLULAR CONSEQUENCES OF SHOCK

The common pathway leading to death from almost any other cause other than instant destruction, occurs within the cell. The body's compensatory mechanisms have developed to preserve cellular function, particularly in vital organs such as the brain, heart and skeletal muscle. As these mechanisms are overwhelmed, cellular and subsequent organ failure ensues. A continuing energy supply is essential for cell survival. All cells do not respond uniformly to shock because cellular energy supply and demands vary, depending on their location in relation to blood supply and their endogenous carbohydrate reserves. For example, although the brain can carry out anaerobic glycolysis it has no glycogen stores and thus depends on a continual supply of glucose via the circulation, and will not survive more than a few minutes of circulatory failure. In contrast, liver and skeletal muscle can survive more prolonged ischaemia because of their capacity to carry out endogenous glycogenolysis. Generation of adenosine triphosphate (ATP) is related to energy demands and changes minute by minute, and although an adult may synthesise about 50kg of ATP each day, the intracellular reserve is very small. This is also true of creatine phosphate, another high energy source found in skeletal muscle, which is rapidly depleted during vigorous exercise. Thus the interruption in energy generation is the most important intracellular event in shock. Substrates which can be used to generate high energy phosphate bonds are glucose and other sugars, fatty acids, ketones, glycerol and amino acids.

Different tissues preferentially utilise substrates to a varying degree, for example the brain metabolises predominantly glucose, the liver and kidney fatty acids, while skeletal muscle metabolises fatty acids under aerobic conditions, but uses its glycogen stores anaerobically for glycogeneolysis during periods of hypoxia. Muscle glycogen is degraded to glucose 6-phosphate (not glucose) which enters the glycolytic pathway, while in liver and kidney glycogenolysis releases glucose which either enters the circulation or undergoes glycolysis via glucose 6-phosphate. Protons and their attendant electrons are transferred from substrates to primary acceptors such as oxidised nicotinamide adenine dinucleotide (NAD^+) or flavin adenine dinucleotide (FAD^+). The major (95%) source of energy in the cell is the oxidation of these electron acceptors in the mitochondria, and it is this intracellular organelle which is the most sensitive to hypoxia and perfusion failure. Electrons from reduced nicotinamide adenine dinucleotide (NADH) or flavin adenine dinucleotide (FADH), are transferred to a series of further electron acceptors within the mitochondrion, with oxygen as the final 'electron sink' leading to the formation of water. Interruption of cellular perfusion results in reduced supply of oxygen and glucose and other substrates and a marked reduction in aerobic energy production.

The immediate effect of cellular hypoxia is a reduction in electron transport within the mitochondrion, and all electron acceptors such as NAD^+, FAD^+, cytochromes and ubiquinones remain in the reduced state. Twenty minutes after interruption of cellular perfusion, electron microscopy reveals mitochondrial swelling; later there are structural changes in the internal membranes, which may represent the influx of sodium ions, water and calcium ions due to local energy deficits. Mitochondrial ATP falls after 15 minutes of ischaemia, then adenosine diphosphate (ADP) concentrations fall and finally these nucleotides are lost completely from the damaged mitochondrial matrix. The appearance of the mitochondrial aspartate aminotransferase in the peripheral circulation represents large scale mitochondrial destruction in severe shock. The ratio of NAD^+/NADH reflects mitochondrial function, and thus indirectly and non-specifically cellular oxygen utilisation. The ratio of acetoacetate to β-hydroxybutyrate is thought to be NAD^+/NADH dependent and has been used as a marker of hepatic perfusion post transplantation, and this approach may be extended to provide a useful marker of overall tissue oxygen utilisation.

The failure of supply of electron acceptors (NAD^+ and FAD^+) to the tricarboxylic acid cycle means that it rapidly slows and then stops. However, unlike mitochondrial metabolism, the glycolytic pathway in the cytosol continues to function under anaerobic conditions. The decreased availability of NAD^+ due to mitochondrial failure makes conversion of pyruvate (the product of glycolysis) to acetyl coenzyme A impossible, both because this is an NAD^+ dependent reaction, and because oxaloacetate production, necessary for the entry of acetyl coenzyme A into the tricarboxylic acid cycle is also NAD^+ dependent. A source of NAD^+ under hypoxic conditions is the reduction of pyruvate to lactate by lactate dehydrogenase. Low intracellular ATP concentrations stimulate glycolysis, thus pyruvate and subsequently lactate concentrations rise. Anaerobic glycolysis of one mole of glucose only produces 2 moles of ATP, compared with 6 moles of ATP during aerobic glycolysis and 36 moles of ATP generated when a molecule of glucose is completely oxidised to CO_2 and H_2O. Anaerobic glycolysis can continue until lactate concentrations become so high that further glycolysis is inhibited.

PLASMA MEMBRANE

Changes in the membrane structure have been well described following shock: the maintenance of the phospholipid bilayer is an energy consuming process. Recent studies suggest that during periods of energy deficit, deformations or 'blebs' appear in the cell membrane, which revert to normal on restoration of adequate energy supply. In low energy states, phosphatidyl serine which is normally kept on the inner membrane leaflet, becomes exposed and appears to activate complement and other components of the acute inflammatory response. After 60 minutes of anoxia, membrane distortion is visible by electron microscopy, with multiple 'blebs' appearing on most cell membranes. After 4 hours anoxia, irreversible membrane deformation takes place. Measurement of membrane potentials in experimental shock indicates that there is a net efflux of potassium ions from, and influx of sodium ions into the cell. The shortage of ATP to power membrane-bound sodium / potassium pumps is probably the key factor to these electrolyte shifts, and has been proposed as the explanation for the frequent finding of hyponatraemia and hyperkalaemia in severe illness, termed the 'sick cell syndrome'. Parallel influxes of calcium and effluxes of magnesium may also occur.

The distortion of the plasma membrane renders membrane-bound receptor sites for hormones such as glucagon and insulin unresponsive, which may partly explain the 'hormone resistance' seen in the critically ill. The cells becomes progressively oedematous due to increased membrane permeability and the influx of water and sodium. As the plasma membrane becomes gradually ineffective, components of the cytosol of increasingly large molecular weight begin to leak into the extracellular fluid, explaining the patterns of enzyme release from organs following shock, such as the isoenzymes of aspartate aminotransferase. Finally the membrane ruptures and cytosol and intracellular organelles are lost into the extracellular space.

NUCLEUS AND ENDOPLASMIC RETICULUM

Following haemorrhagic shock, chromatin becomes clumped and marginated around the edge of the nucleus. Both smooth and rough endoplasmic reticulum become swollen, and in irreversible shock ribosomes become detached from the endoplasmic reticulum. The activity of RNA polymerase is decreased, and what RNA is synthesised is of lower molecular weight than normal. The whole of the protein synthetic chain within the cell is either reduced in activity or dislocated altogether. Since maintenance of the integrity of subcellular organelles and protein synthesis itself is an energy-consuming process, these changes may reflect the reduced energy production. However, in surviving cells incorporation of amino acids into proteins post shock can take days or even weeks to return to normal. It is interesting to note that skin biopsies taken from severe burn victims for in-vitro culture, must be taken within 24 hours of the injury, as after this time the cells fail to multiply adequately. The explanation is not clear but may be related to the effects of shock on protein synthesis in surviving cells.

LYSOSOMES

In the early post shock period lysosomes appear unaffected, and only in the later stages are lysosomal membranes seen to rupture. It may be that lysosomal rupture and the release of lysosomal enzymes into the cytosol represent an irreversible step leading to cell death. A fall in intracellular pH due to lactic acid accumulation appears to be one of the mechanisms leading to lysosomal rupture.

FURTHER READING

Baue AE Physiology of shock and injury. In: Shock and resuscitation. Geller E (ed) R McGraw-Hill,Inc. Health Professions Division. New York 1993; 67-126.

Haljamäe H The pathophysiology os shock. In: Shock and shock treatment. J Acta Anaesthesiologia Scandinavica. (1993) Supplement 98, **37**; 3-6.

Rush BF Biochemical and cellular pathology of shock. In: Hardaway RM (ed). Shock the reversible stage of dying. PSG Publishing Co Inc. Massachusetts 1988; 68-77.

Chapter 2

Delivery of and utilisation of cellular nutrients in shock

INTRODUCTION

The primary aim of the management of the critically ill is to provide appropriate nutrients in adequate quantities to the cells that need them. Achieving this requires a rational approach to therapy which in turn requires an understanding of which nutrients are important, the mechanism by which they normally reach the cells and how this process can be effectively monitored. This topic can be considered in three parts:

- which nutrients are important
- how much of a nutrient is needed
- how the nutrients are made available where required.

Oxygen is the single most important nutrient and will be discussed in detail since the general principles relating to its provision to the cells can be extended to all the other nutrients. Shock can be considered as a failure to provide the cells with adequate nutrients. As nutrients are transported by the cardiovascular system, normal cardiovascular physiology and the pathophysiology of shock will be discussed together with measurements pertaining to the diagnosis and management of shock.

NORMAL CARDIOVASCULAR PHYSIOLOGY

The cardiovascular system consists of two pumps, the left and right ventricles, connected in series by blood vessels. The left ventricle pumps blood to the major organs through the systemic circulation, while the right ventricle pumps blood to the lungs through the pulmonary circulation. Blood flows around this circuit from regions of high hydrostatic pressure to regions where the pressure is lower. The rate of flow depends on the pressure gradient along the vessel and its cross sectional area. Flow rate increases with a rise in pressure gradient or an increase in cross sectional area. The resistance to flow is inversely related to the bore of the vessel.

$$\text{flow rate} = \frac{\text{pressure gradient}}{\text{resistance}}$$

In critically ill patients, a low systemic blood pressure is often the precipitating reason for investigation and therapy of derangements of the cardiovascular system. Therefore the above equation is often rearranged.

$$\text{pressure gradient} = \text{flow rate x resistance}$$

The flow rate is the cardiac output. In the systemic circulation, the driving pressure is the difference between the mean arterial pressure (MAP) and the pressure in the right atrium i.e., the central venous pressure (CVP), and the resistance is termed the systemic vascular resistance (SVR). In the pulmonary circulation, the driving pressure is the difference between the mean pulmonary artery pressure (MPAP) and the pressure in the left atrium and the resistance is termed the pulmonary vascular resistance (PVR). Left atrial pressure can only be measured by surgically opening the chest and inserting a cannula into the left atrium which is applicable only during cardiac surgery and not in a general ITU. The wedge pressure, also known as the pulmonary artery occlusion pressure (PAOP), is used to estimate the left atrial pressure. In practice the PAOP is measured by wedging a pulmonary artery catheter in a small pulmonary artery by inflating a balloon on its tip. The pressure measured from the tip of the catheter will then equilibrate with the left atrium to give the wedge pressure. An example of normal values and calculations is shown in Table 2.1.

The SVR is determined primarily by the calibre of the arterioles, which is affected by neural, humoral and local factors. The vasomotor centre in the brain exerts overall control of the resistance by acting through the autonomic nervous system to divert blood to appropriate organs. The resistance of individual arterioles can also be influenced by local factors such as the products of metabolism, including carbon dioxide, hydrogen ions, potassium ions and histamine, all of which cause local

Table 2.1 Normal pressures in the cardiovascular system

- Cardiac output (CO) 5 L/min
- Mean arterial pressure (MAP) 90 mmHg
- Central venous pressure (CVP) 5 mmHg
- Mean pulmonary artery pressure (MPAP) 12 mmHg
- Pulmonary artery occlusion pressure (PAOP) 8 mmHg
- Constant to convert mmHg .sec/L to dyne.sec.cm^{-5} 80
- Systemic vascular resistance (SVR) $= \frac{MAP - CVP}{CO} \times \text{constant}$

$$= \frac{90 - 5}{5} \times 80$$

$$= 1360 \text{ dyne.sec.cm}^{-5}$$

- Pulmonary vascular resistance (PVR) $= \frac{MPAP - PAOP}{CO} \times \text{constant}$

$$= \frac{12 - 8}{5} \times 80$$

$$= 64 \text{ dyne.sec.cm}^{-5}$$

vasodilatation. The humoral factors include the adrenaline released from the adrenal gland.

In the normal stresses of daily living different tissues have different requirements. For instance, when exercising, blood is directed to the muscles doing the work while being diverted from elsewhere. When the total flow is inadequate to perfuse all tissues, the body has protective mechanisms to preserve flow to vital organs such as the brain, heart and kidneys while decreasing flow to organs whose nutrient requirements are less immediate, such as the skin. This control of blood flow is effected by vasoconstriction and vasodilatation to the vessels of various organs. Normally not all capillaries are perfused all the time and mast cells release histamine which leads to capillary vasodilatation. When perfusion is adequate the histamine release declines and there is subsequent vasoconstriction until the mast cells release more histamine and the cycle is repeated. Complete vasodilatation can increase the volume of the vascular tree threefold. Blood can bypass the capillaries through variable arteriolar venular shunts. When these shunts open nutrients in arterial blood will not reach the capillaries or the intended tissues (Fig 2.1).

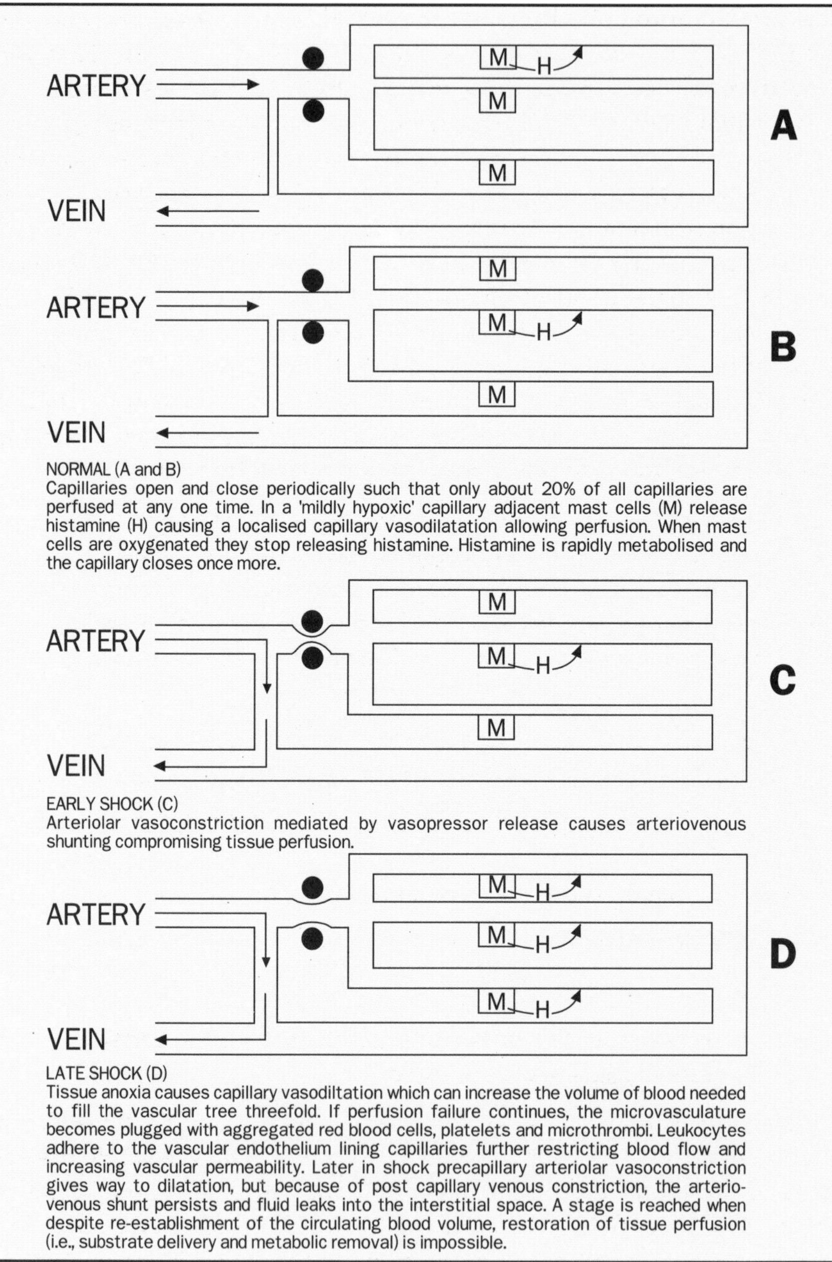

Fig 2.1 Effect of vasodilatation and vasoconstriction on microcirculation in shock

The cardiac output is the total amount of blood passing around the circulation per unit time and is normally about 5 L/min. It is the product of the heart rate and the stroke volume. The intrinsic rate of the heart is about 120 beats per minute but is normally only 80 because the heart is slowed by the action of the parasympathetic nervous system, through the vagus nerve. The heart rate rises with decreased vagal activity, stimulation of the sympathetic nervous system, or increased levels of circulating catecholamines such as adrenaline. The stroke volume (SV) is the amount of blood ejected from the ventricle with each heart beat and is normally about 70 mL. The SV is the difference between the ventricular volume at the end of diastole (EDV), when the ventricle has finished filling, and the ventricular volume at the end of systole (ESV), when it has finished emptying. The volume of venous blood entering the ventricle via the atria depends on several factors.

- The hydrostatic pressure is higher in the veins than in the ventricle during diastole and this drives the blood into the ventricle. The venous pressure is determined by the balance between the volume of blood in the circulation and the size of the vessels. Constriction of the vessels results in a higher pressure for a given volume.
- The ventricular compliance is the volume of blood that can be contained in the ventricle at a specified pressure. A compliant ventricle has a larger volume than a non-compliant one.
- Anatomically there is a maximum volume.

The ESV depends on:

- The contractility of the heart.
- The resistance of the vessels into which the blood is ejected, the systemic vascular resistance (SVR).

Contractility is defined as the force with which a muscle contracts in relation to the load that is placed on it. A normal ventricle is able to eject most of the blood presented to it from the veins. As more blood is returned to the ventricle, the more the ventricular muscle is stretched so that the next contraction is more forceful and the extra blood is ejected.

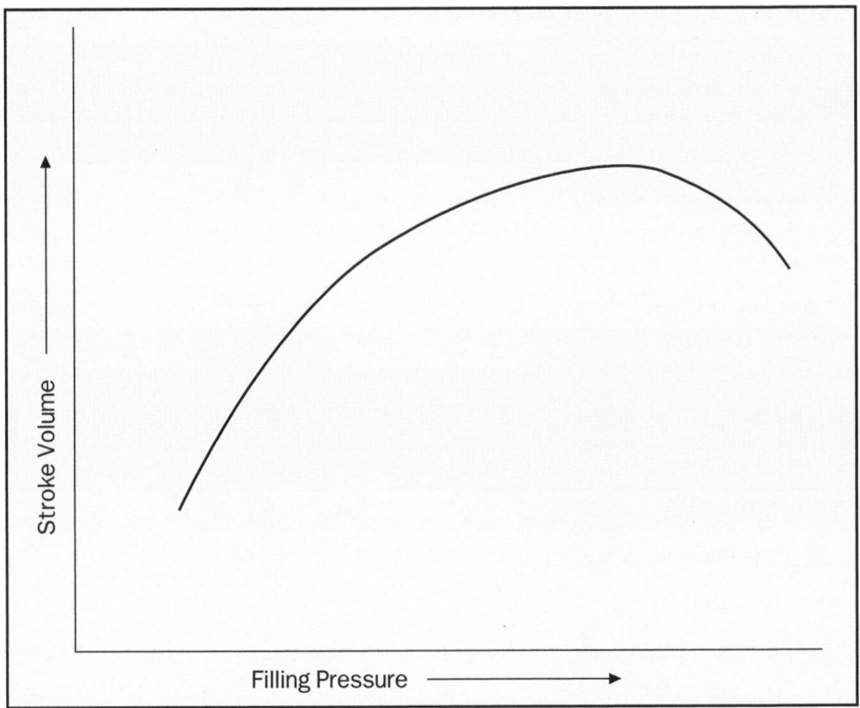

Fig 2.2 Starling's Law of the heart.
The effect of filling pressure on the stroke volume of the heart. Filling pressure depends upon end diastolic pressure, pulmonary artery occlusion pressure and central venous pressure.

This is known as Starlings 'Law of the Heart' (Fig 2.2). It is analogous to stretching an elastic band and then releasing it. The more the elastic band is stretched, the greater force with which it contracts when released. However, when the stretch is maximal, any further stretch does not increase the subsequent force of contraction. Any further stretching may cause a decrease of the force of contraction. The heart fails when the extra stretch reduces the cardiac output. Heart muscle is unique because its contractility varies. This ability to change the contractility is analogous to changing the elastic band. The contractility is affected by the sympathetic nervous system and circulating hormones such as adrenaline (see Chapter 3 p102). Usually the SVR has little influence on

Table 2.2 Broad categories of hypotension

Category	Haemodynamic changes*		
	Resistance	**Cardiac output**	**CVP/PAOP**
Cardiogenic	high	**LOW**	high
Hypovolaemia	high	low/normal	**LOW**
Vasodilatatory	**LOW**	high/normal	low

*Primary event in capitals

the cardiac output because the heart has sufficient reserves of power to generate the required pressures. However, when the heart fails then either the output or the pressure will fall.

Hypotension has many clinical causes but consideration of the physiology narrows these to three broad categories (Table 2.2)

- cardiogenic
- hypovolaemic
- vasodilatatory.

Hypotension will be due to either a fall in systemic vascular resistance or cardiac output. If the MAP falls to 45 mmHg with a normal cardiac output of 5 L/min and a CVP of 5 mmHg, then the SVR will fall to 640 dyne.sec.cm^{-5}. Whereas if the MAP falls to 45 mmHg and the SVR remains normal at 1360 dyne.sec.cm^{-5}, then the cardiac output has to have fallen to 2.5 L/min. The overall control mechanisms of the cardiovascular system act primarily to maintain the blood pressure. Therefore when the MAP falls, the control system tries to maintain it by increasing the SVR and the cardiac output. The vasomotor centre collates information about the MAP from the baroreceptors and makes adjustments via the autonomic nervous system to the SVR and the cardiac output.

In hypovolaemic shock, the primary problem is an inadequate circulating volume (with a low CVP and PAOP) resulting in inadequate filling of the ventricle and a fall in cardiac output. The fall in cardiac output causes a fall in MAP which is detected by the baroreceptors. These relay the information to the vasomotor centre which increases sympathetic activity. This causes vasoconstriction with a rise in SVR and maintenance of the MAP unless the hypovolaemia is severe in which case defences fail and the MAP continues to fall.

Table 2.3 Summary of cardiovascular physiology

- MAP = CO × SVR
- CO = HR × SV
- SV = EDV – ESV

MAP mean arterial pressure	HR heart rate
CO cardiac output	SV stroke volume
SVR systemic vascular resistance	EDV end diastolic volume
	ESV end systolic volume

In septic shock, vasodilatation causes a fall in SVR and thus MAP falls. This is detected by the baroreceptors and relayed to the vasomotor centre with a resultant increase in sympathetic activity. This will increase cardiac output and if the heart has sufficient reserves then the MAP may return to normal. The vasodilatation may also result in pooling of blood in peripherally dilated vessels and cause a relative hypovolaemia (with a low CVP and PAOP).

In cardiogenic shock, the primary problem is a fall in myocardial contractility and a fall in cardiac output as the heart fails to eject the blood returned to it (with a high CVP and PAOP). The MAP fall is detected by the baroreceptors which relay the information to the vasomotor centre which increases sympathetic activity. This causes a vasoconstriction with a rise in SVR and maintenance of the BP (Table 2.3).

Hypotension in shock is often caused by a combination of two or even all three categories of cardiovascular failure. However, an understanding of the principles allows a logical approach to managing individual patients

OXYGEN

DELIVERY OF OXYGEN

The supply of oxygen to the cells is a complex process depending on an adequate oxygen content of inspired gas, adequate respiratory function, adequate cardiovascular transport and normal cellular uptake. Each stage will be considered in detail, except the cardiovascular, which has already been covered.

ATMOSPHERE TO ALVEOLI

Oxygen reaches the terminal bronchioles by bulk gas flow and then diffuses into the alveoli. All the alveolar oxygen is in the gaseous phase and therefore the volume of alveolar oxygen is directly proportional to oxygen tension. The alveolar oxygen tension (P_AO_2) can be derived from equation 1.

$$P_AO_2 = FiO_2 \times (PB - PH_2O) - P_ACO_2/RQ \qquad \textbf{Eq. 1}$$

The P_AO_2 depends on the inspired oxygen fraction (FiO_2), the barometric pressure (PB), the alveolar water vapour pressure (PH_2O), the alveolar carbon dioxide tension (P_ACO_2), and the respiratory quotient (RQ). The respiratory quotient is included because volume for volume the body's consumption of oxygen is greater than its production of carbon dioxide (normally 250 and 200 mL/min respectively). The P_ACO_2 is not usually measured and for calculation purposes it is assumed to be the same as the arterial carbon dioxide tension (PaO_2). The barometric pressure is determined by altitude and meteorological factors, while the water vapour pressure is 6.3 kPa at 37°C.

EFFECT OF CHANGES IN FiO_2 AND P_ACO_2

The FiO_2 of air is about 0.21 which can be increased to a maximum of 1.0 by adding oxygen to the inspired gases. In the presence of normal P_ACO_2 (5.3 kPa), PB (101 kPa), PH_2O (6.3 kPa), and RQ (0.8) the P_AO_2 will rise from 13.3 to 88.1 kPa when the FiO_2 is increased from 0.21 to 1.0 (Eq. 2 & 3).

IF:

$FiO_2 = 0.21$ $\quad P_AO_2 = 0.21 \times (101-6.3) - 5.3/0.8$

$P_ACO_2 = 5.3$ $\quad = 13.3$ **Eq. 2**

IF.

$FiO_2 = 1.0$ $\quad P_AO_2 = 1.0 \times (101-6.3) - 5.3/0.8$

$P_ACO_2 = 5.3$ $\quad = 88.1$ **Eq. 3**

The carbon dioxide level in the alveoli is determined by the balance between that produced from metabolism and that removed by ventilation (Eq. 4). An increase in production will raise the $P_{A}CO_2$ while an increase in removal will lower the $P_{A}CO_2$.

$$P_{A}CO_2 = \frac{CO_2 \text{ production}}{\text{alveolar ventilation}} \qquad \textbf{Eq. 4}$$

The $P_{A}CO_2$ has a clinically significant effect on the $P_{A}O_2$ only with a normal FiO_2 of 0.21. This is illustrated below where the $P_{A}CO_2$ is increased from the normal 5.3 to 10 kPa with an FiO_2 of 0.21 and 1.0 (Eqs. 2, 3, 5 & 6).

IF:

$FiO_2 = 0.21$ $\qquad P_{A}O_2 = 0.21 \times (101 - 6.3) - 10/0.8$

$P_{A}CO_2 = 10$ $\qquad = 7.4$ $\qquad$ **Eq. 5**

IF:

$FiO_2 = 1.0$ $\qquad P_{A}O_2 = 1.0 \times (101 - 6.3) - 10/0.8$

$P_{A}CO_2 = 10$ $\qquad = 82.2$ $\qquad$ **Eq. 6**

The doubling of $P_{A}CO_2$ almost halves the $P_{A}O_2$ at an FiO_2 of 0.21 yet produces no clinically significant effect at an FiO_2 of 1.0.

ALVEOLI TO BLOOD

Oxygen diffuses from the alveolar space through the alveolar-capillary membrane and dissolves in the plasma. At a normal arterial oxygen tension (PaO_2) of 13 kPa, a litre of plasma contains about 3 mL of oxygen. Were it not for the presence of haemoglobin, a minimum of 83 L/min of plasma would be needed to meet the body's normal oxygen requirement of 250 mL/min. Oxygen diffuses from the plasma into the red blood cells to combine with haemoglobin (Hb) to form oxyhaemoglobin (HbO_2). The movement of oxygen from the plasma causes the tension to fall and more oxygen diffuses from the alveoli into the plasma. This continues until an equilibrium is reached or the blood flows on. The saturation (SO_2) is the percentage of the Hb present as

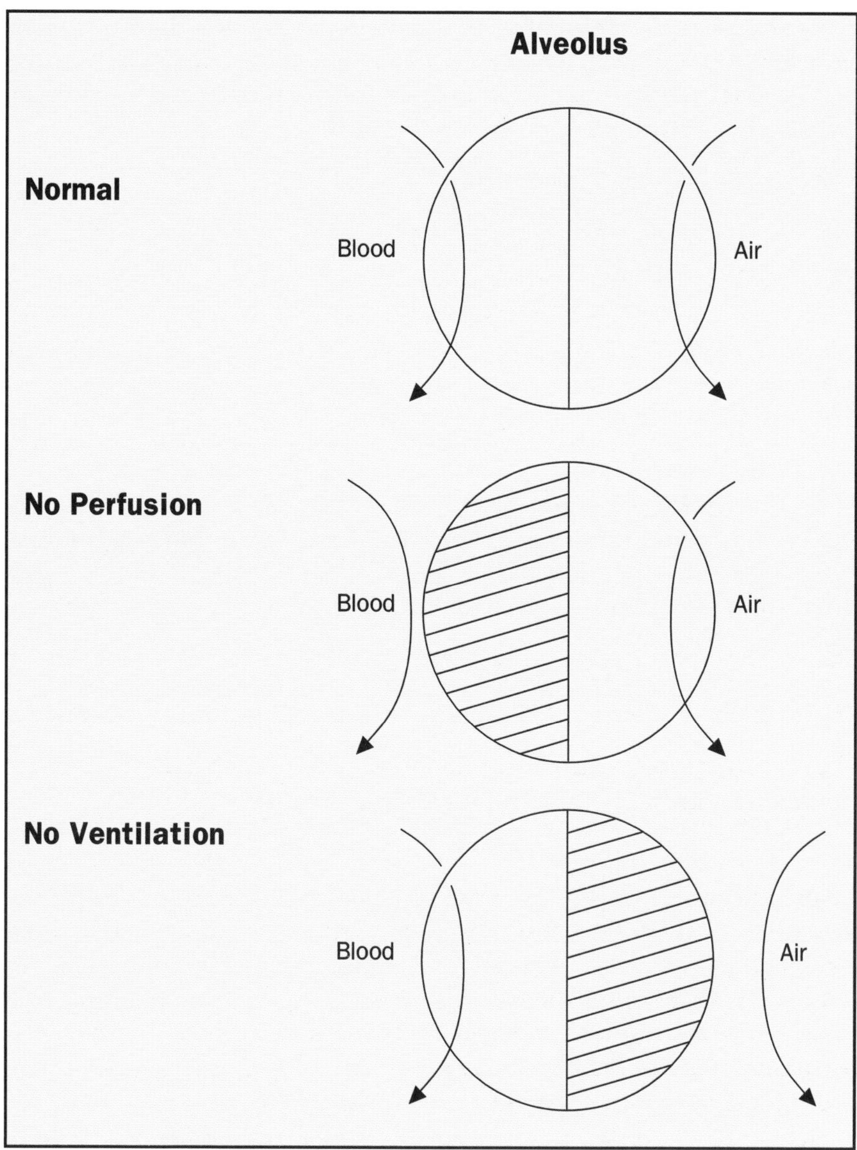

Fig 2.3 **Intra Pulmonary shunting. Most alveoli are normally perfused with blood. However some ventilated alveoli are not perfused (dead space) and alveoli are perfused but not ventilated (shunt) see page 20.**

HbO_2. Each gram of Hb can carry a theoretical maximum of 1.39 mL of oxygen (the Hufner factor). The volume of oxygen carried in the blood, the content, is the sum of oxygen combined with Hb and oxygen dissolved in the plasma (Eq. 7).

$$\text{oxygen content (mL/L)} = \frac{(Hb \times SO_2 \times 1.39)}{100} + (PO_2 \times 0.23) \qquad \textbf{Eq. 7}$$

Where:

PO_2 is the dissolved oxygen tension (kPa)

0.23 is the volume of dissolved oxygen (mL/L) for each kPa PO_2

Hb is the haemoglobin concentration (g/L)

INTRA PULMONARY SHUNTS

If all the alveoli were perfectly ventilated and perfectly perfused, the arterial blood would have the same composition as the blood leaving the alveoli (end capillary blood). However, some blood perfuses the lungs without coming into contact with alveolar gas (shunt) whilst some ventilated alveoli are not perfused (dead space) (Fig 2.3). The shunted blood mixes with the end capillary blood to become arterial blood. In normal people there is a small shunt due to mismatching of ventilation and perfusion, which usually increases in critically ill patients with respiratory problems. Inadequate ventilation of alveoli may be due to their collapse or being filled with fluid. The increased shunt causes a fall in arterial oxygen content and PaO_2 (Eq. 8).

$$CaO_2 = CcO_2 \times (1\text{-}sf) + (CvO_2 \times sf) \qquad \textbf{Eq. 8}$$

Where:

CaO_2	arterial oxygen content
CcO_2	end capillary oxygen content
CvO_2	mixed venous content
sf	fraction of the flow bypassing the alveoli

With no shunt (sf = 0) the arterial blood has the same oxygen content as the end capillary blood and the PaO_2 will equal the P_AO_2. As the shunt increases, with no change in CcO_2 or CvO_2, the CaO_2 will fall and the PaO_2 will be less than the P_AO_2. The fall in PaO_2 with an increase in shunt

Table 2.4 Effect of FiO_2 of 0.21 and 0.50 on the arterial PO_2 with shunts of 10% and 50%

FiO_2	End-capillary		Arterial	
	PO_2 (kPa)	Sat (%)	PO_2 (kPa)	Sat (%)
	50% shunt with venous saturation of 75%			
0.21	14	97.5	6.7	85.5
0.50	40	100	7.0	87.5
	10% shunt with venous saturation of 75%			
0.21	14	97.5	10	93.9
0.50	40	100	14	97.5

is not linear because of the sigmoid relationship of PO_2 to blood oxygen content. As most of the oxygen is carried as HbO_2 the smaller dissolved fraction can be ignored for the purposes of the following explanation. In Eq. 8, CaO_2, CcO_2 and CvO_2 each relate to the same Hb concentration and Hufner factor and when eliminated give Eq. 9.

$$SaO_2 = ScO_2 \text{ x } (1\text{-sf}) + (SvO_2 \times \text{sf}) \qquad \textbf{Eq. 9}$$

Where:

SaO_2 arterial oxygen saturation
ScO_2 end capillary oxygen saturation
SvO_2 mixed venous oxygen saturation

With no shunt (sf=0) the SaO_2 equals the ScO_2, which with an FiO_2 0.21 would be about 96%. With a 50% shunt (sf=0.5), SvO_2 75%, and FiO_2 0.21 the SaO_2 would be about 85.5%. Increasing the FiO_2 to 1.0 would raise the ScO_2 to 100% and with the SvO_2 staying 75%, the SaO_2 would rise to 87.5%, an increase of only 2%. Inspection of the oxygen dissociation curve (Fig 2.4) shows that this is only a small increase in PaO_2. This illustrates why a low PaO_2, that is due to a large shunt, cannot be successfully treated by increasing FiO_2 alone (Table 2.4).

TOTAL OXYGEN DELIVERY

The cardiovascular system transports oxygenated blood from the lungs to the tissues and returns deoxygenated blood to the lungs. The total oxygen delivery is the product of the arterial blood oxygen content and the cardiac output (Eq. 10).

$$DO_2 = CaO_2 \times CO \qquad \textbf{Eq. 10}$$

Where:

DO_2	Oxygen delivery (mL/min)
CaO_2	Arterial oxygen content (mL/L)
CO	Cardiac output (L/min)

TOTAL OXYGEN CONSUMPTION

The oxygen consumption is the difference between the oxygen delivered to the tissues and the oxygen returned to the pulmonary artery as mixed venous blood (Eq. 11).

$$\dot{V}O_2 = (CaO_2 \times CO) - (CvO_2 \times CO)$$
$$= (CaO_2 - CvO_2) \times CO \qquad \textbf{Eq. 11}$$

Where:

$\dot{V}O_2$	Oxygen consumption (mL/min)
CaO_2	Arterial oxygen content (mL/L)
CvO_2	Mixed venous oxygen content (mL/L)
CO	Cardiac output (L/min)

MEASUREMENT OF OXYGEN CONTENT, DELIVERY AND CONSUMPTION

Before measurements are made to assess oxygenation status it is essential that the sample has been properly collected, stored and transported. These issues are discussed in Chapter 5.

Van Slyke described a direct method for measuring oxygen content in 1924. The principle of this method is to liberate all the oxygen from the blood sample and measure its volume. However, it is a time consuming technique that requires experienced laboratory staff to produce reliable and accurate results. It is a technique that does not lend itself to automation and is now usually reserved for research as it is still considered the "gold standard". Other methods of direct measurement of the oxygen content of blood have been described but have not gained widespread acceptance. In clinical practice, oxygen content is derived from Eq. 7 after measurement of Hb, PO_2 and haemoglobin saturation (SO_2).

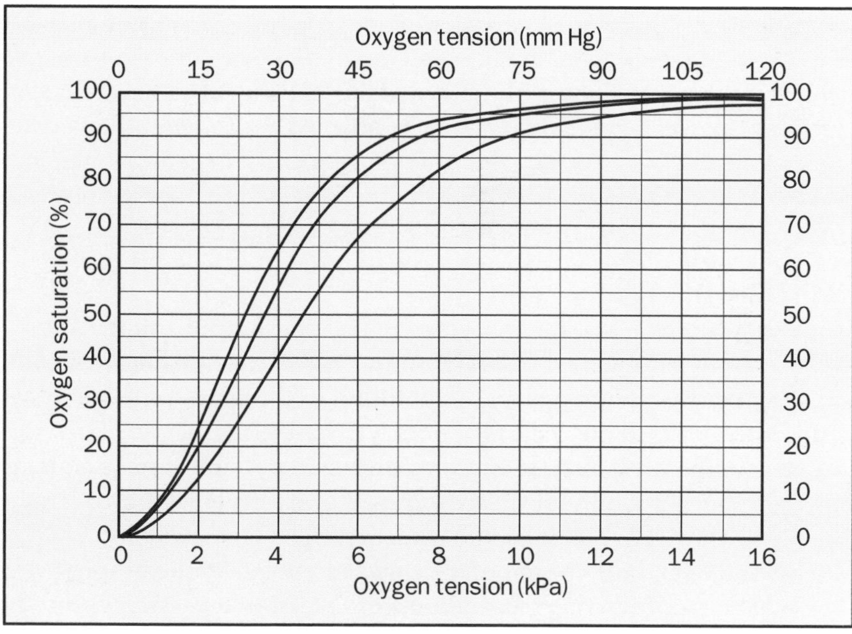

Fig 2.4 Oxygen dissociation curve.
An increase in carbon dioxide, hydrogen ion concentration, temperature and 2,3-diphosphoglycerate will shift the curve to the right, while a decrease will move the curve to the left

Hb saturation can be reported in two ways, either as a percentage of the total Hb or as a percentage of Hb available for oxygen transport i.e., the sum of oxygenated and reduced Hb. If all the Hb was available to carry oxygen, each gram could theoretically accommodate 1.39 mL of oxygen. However, when Hufner measured the oxygen carried by Hb he found each gram carried 1.34 mL of oxygen. This figure probably reflects all the Hb moieties, including small proportions of Hb that cannot carry oxygen such as carboxyhaemoglobin and methaemoglobin. Oximeters are capable of measuring the SO_2 and Hb accurately and rapidly. An alternative is to derive the SO_2 from the PO_2 and the oxygen dissociation curve (ODC). The ODC is sigmoid because each Hb molecule can combine with four oxygen molecules and the ease with which each attaches varies. However, calculated SO_2 is unreliable because the shape and the position of the ODC can be changed by physiological and pathological conditions. An increase in carbon dioxide, hydrogen ions, temperature and 2,3- diphosphoglycerate (2,3-DPG) will shift the curve to the right, while a decrease will move the curve to the left (Fig 2.4). This method of deriving oxygen content has been confirmed as unreliable even for normal adults. As critically ill patients frequently have derangements likely to displace the ODC, calculated SO_2 errors are even more likely and deriving contents from a calculated SO_2 cannot be recommended.

OXYGEN DELIVERY

The oxygen delivery is the product of the cardiac output and the arterial oxygen content (Eq. 10). Cardiac output can be measured invasively utilising the Fick principle, by dye dilution or thermodilution. This can either be intermittently or continuously. The Fick principle states that the amount of substance taken up by an organ per unit time is equal to the arterial level of the substance minus the venous level multiplied by the blood flow (Eq. 11). It can be measured non-invasively by Doppler ultrasound techniques or impedance measurements of the thoracic cavity, which can be either continuous or intermittent. At present the accepted standard technique is the thermodilution method. This requires the insertion of a catheter into the pulmonary artery and can only be safely offered in units specialising in the technique. The latest pulmonary artery catheters allow continuous measurements of cardiac output or mixed venous saturation.

HOW MUCH OXYGEN IS ENOUGH ?

The simple answer to this question is when each cell gets enough oxygen to meet the demand. The difficulty is to identify when this occurs and when it does not. Since it is not yet possible to monitor individually each cell or even each organ, cruder methods of determining total body oxygen requirements are used.

Since the introduction of the Clarke electrode, usual teaching has been that PaO_2 of greater than 9.3 kPa is adequate. This value is associated with a near maximal saturation of Hb, and thus content assuming a normal ODC. The position of the ODC is not fixed and when displaced to the right, a higher PO_2 is required to maintain the same saturation. The P50 is the tension at which Hb is 50% saturated (normal 3.65 kPa) and is the usual way of describing the position of the ODC. An alterna-

Table 2.5 The arterio- venous oxygen content difference when the ODC is shifted to the right with no change in the PaO_2 or PvO_2.

				Oxygen Contents mL/L		Tissue uptake mL/L
PO_2	SO_2	Hb (g/L)	Shift	Arterial	Venous	
100	95.1	10	Normal	133	42	91
100	90	10	Right	125	26	99

Venous content is based on an assumed PvO_2 of 2.7 kPa.

tive is to consider the PO_2 at 95% saturation, the P95. A single measurement of PO_2 and SO_2 can be used to calculate the position. This is achieved by comparing the measured PO_2 with the PO_2 calculated from the measured SO_2 on a normally placed ODC. This can be done either graphically with a series of ODCs or mathematically.

At first glance, a right shifted ODC suggests decreased oxygen availability to the tissues because the arterial content will be lower for a given PO_2. However at the cellular level availability increases because more oxygen is liberated for a given capillary PO_2. The mitochondria need a minimum PO_2 of 0.0026-0.0039 kPa to function and the capillary PO_2needs to be a minimum of 2.7 kPa for the oxygen to diffuse to the mitochondria. The oxygen made available by decreasing the PO_2 from arterial to 2.7 kPa reveals that more oxygen is released when the ODC is shifted to the right (Table 2.5). Calculation of this *theoretical conditional extraction* is a method of integrating the PO_2, the Hb, the SO_2 and ODC position in a single parameter.

Detection of arterial hypoxia has been made easier by introduction of affordable non invasive pulse oximetry. The pulse oximeter works on the same principles as blood oximetry but shines the light through tissue such as a finger or an ear lobe. It is able to separate the background signals from that of the arterial pulse (see Chapter 5). Pulse oximetry is inaccurate at low saturations and the values may vary between machines. Readings are dependent on good perfusion of the tissues being monitored and may be misleading in patients in shock. Furthermore pulse oximetry gives no indication of the acid-base status, PCO_2, or the Hb concentration.

LACTATE

When the oxygen delivery does not meet the demand, metabolism changes from aerobic to anaerobic in those tissues which normally exist by aerobic metabolism. Pyruvate is converted into lactate rather than into carbon dioxide and water via Krebs' cycle. A rise in blood lactate concentration is thus indirect evidence of inadequate oxygen delivery. In a study group of shocked patients, a blood lactate >5.7 mmol/L was found to be associated with a 100% mortality. Unfortunately, a rising blood lactate is a late feature of tissue hypoxia; by the time it is detected irreparable cellular damage may have occurred. Its place in managing individual patients in the ITU still requires further study.

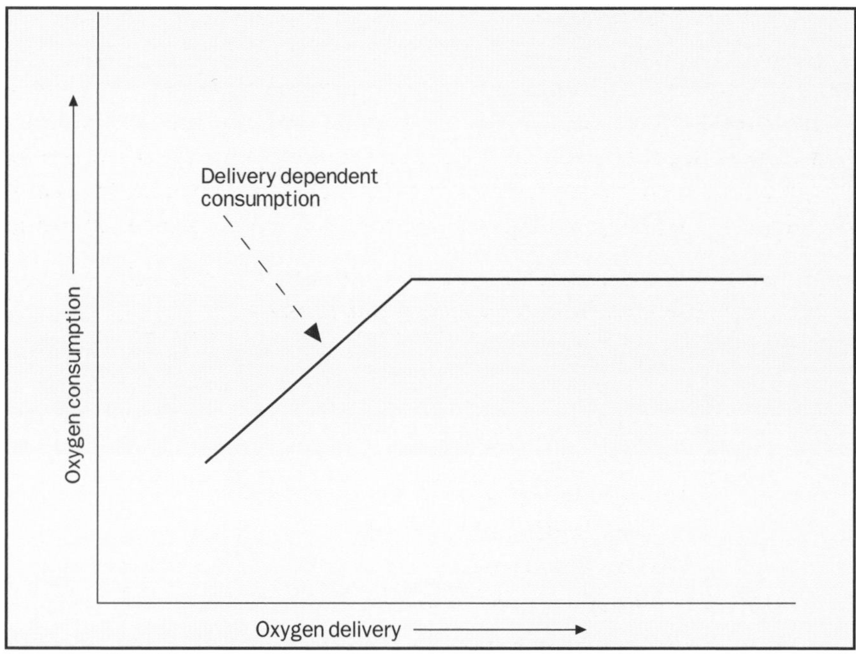

Fig 2.5 Delivery dependent oxygen consumption

DELIVERY DEPENDENT OXYGEN CONSUMPTION

Oxygen delivery to the tissues is normally in excess of requirements and a decrease in delivery is met by relatively more oxygen being extracted from the blood. However, a point is reached when any further decrease in oxygen delivery cannot be matched by an increase in extraction and the oxygen consumption falls and becomes delivery dependent (Fig 2.5). This has been demonstrated in animals by decreasing delivery and reported in anaesthetized patients prior to cardio-pulmonary bypass operations. In critically ill patients, delivery dependent oxygen consumption has been more difficult to demonstrate. It has been suggested that therapy could be directed to increasing the delivery until consumption is maximal. This is an attractive idea but has yet to be reported to influence patient outcome.

CLINICAL OUTCOME

Shoemaker and colleagues measured serially a large number of physiological variables in critically ill post-operative patients. The variables were ranked according to their ability to predict survival. The two most important predictors of survival were circulating blood volume and cardiac output. The next two most important predictors were a supranormal oxygen delivery and a supranormal oxygen consumption. It is interesting that PaO_2 and SaO_2, common objective assessments of oxygenation, were poor predictors of outcome. A prospective trial compared a control group managed conventionally with a treatment group

Table 2.6 Guidelines for therapy of critically ill surgical patients in order of temporal priority.

- Blood volume
  - > 2.7 L/M^2 for females
  - > 3.0 L/M^2 for males
- Cardiac index* > 4.5 L/M^2
- O_2 delivery > 550 mL/min/M^2
- O_2 consumption > 167 mL/min/M^2
- Blood pressure normal
- Wedge pressure < 20 mmHg
- Pulmonary vascular resistance < 250 dyne.sec.cm^{-5}.
- $PaO_2 > 9.3$ kPa
- $SaO_2 > 90\%$
- pH >7.3 and <7.5
- $P\bar{v}O_2 > 4.0$ kPa

*Cardiac index is the cardiac output adjusted to patient size by dividing it by the body surface area in square metres

managed by adjusting physiological variables to the supranormal values associated with survival (Table 2.6). The patients were randomly allocated and of equivalent degrees of illness. The treatment group had a mortality of 13% and the control group 48%, which was statistically and clinically significant. A further group of high risk surgical patients had oxygen consumption followed perioperatively . The total oxygen debt was calculated as the difference between measured oxygen consumption and the estimated oxygen requirements. Survivors incurred a lower oxygen debt (26.8 L) than the non-survivors (33.5 L). Furthermore the survivors without organ failure had a lower oxygen debt (8.0 L) than the survivors with organ failure.

These studies support the premise that cellular and organ failure follow inadequate oxygen delivery and utilisation. Furthermore they suggest that adjusting patients' physiological parameters into the range associated with survival can improve outcome.

At present the methods for deriving the data for oxygen delivery and consumption require the use of complex invasive monitoring. Therefore it is necessary to have a rational approach to the monitoring and management of hypoxic patients.

MANAGEMENT OF HYPOXIA

Management of hypoxia can be approached by considering Fig 2.6 and Table 2.7.

The arterial oxygen content and thus the PaO_2 depend on:

- end-capillary content
- mixed venous oxygen content
- degree of shunt (Eq. 8).

As described earlier, the end-capillary oxygen content depends on the alveolar PO_2 and the Hb concentration (Eqs. 1 and 7). Adjustment of the FiO_2 by adding oxygen, the P_ACO2 by ensuring adequate ventilation, and Hb by transfusion, will optimise the end capillary oxygen content.

The shunt fraction can be decreased by improving ventilation of partially and totally collapsed alveoli. These can be re-inflated by applying positive pressure to the airway either as intermittent positive pressure

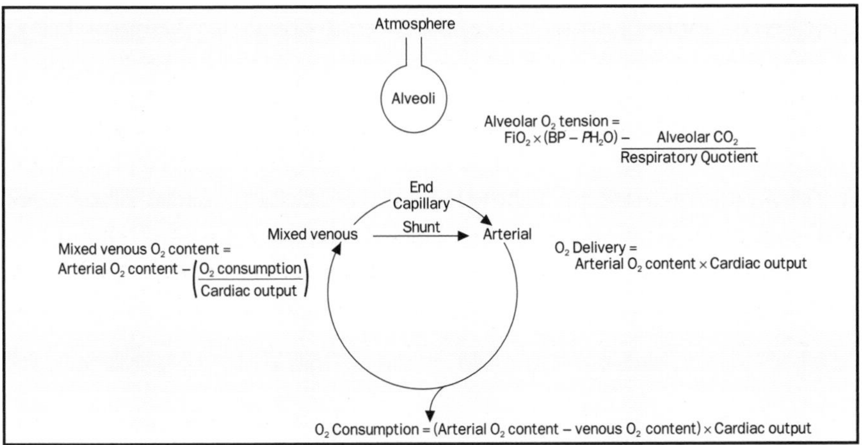

Fig 2.6 Overview of oxygen delivery to tissues.

ventilation (IPPV) with positive end expiratory pressure (PEEP) or by continuous positive airway pressure (CPAP). Unfortunately the application of PEEP/CPAP can decrease the cardiac output, by increasing the intra-thoracic pressure and decreasing the return of blood to the heart. A decrease in cardiac output will decrease the total oxygen delivery. Therefore an increase in arterial oxygen content achieved with PEEP/CPAP has to be balanced against a potential decrease in cardiac output, the aim being to increase the overall oxygen delivery.

Table 2.7 Variables that allow a rational approach to monitoring and managing hypoxia in ITU patients.

Measured Values	Derived values
• FiO_2	Alveolar O_2
• $PaCO_2$	
• Hb	End capillary content
• PaO_2	Arterial content,
	Oxygen dissociation curve position
• SaO_2	Conditional extraction
• SvO_2	Oxygen delivery
• PvO_2	Oxygen consumption
• Cardiac output	

The mixed venous oxygen content is determined by the oxygen delivery and oxygen consumption as shown by rearrangement of Eq. 11.

$$\dot{V}O_2 = CO \times (CaO_2 - CvO_2)$$

$$CvO_2 = CaO_2 - \frac{\dot{V}O_2}{CO} \qquad \textbf{Eq. 12}$$

The mixed venous oxygen content can be increased by :

- increasing the cardiac output
- decreasing the oxygen consumption
- increasing the arterial oxygen content.

OXYGEN TOXICITY

Excess oxygen can cause convulsions, pulmonary damage and retrolental fibroplasia. Convulsions occur when the oxygen tension is greater than two atmospheres. The mechanism is unclear but is associated with decreases in gamma-aminobutyric acid in the brain. Pulmonary damage includes a decrease in type 1 and increase in type 2 alveolar cells, absorption collapse of alveoli, and ventilatory depression. The type 1 cells line the alveoli and are derived from type 2 cells, which do not act as gas exchange membranes.

It appears that it is the oxygen tension rather than its concentration that determines pulmonary toxicity. The use of 100% oxygen at one atmosphere for short periods seems to be safe. On the author's Intensive Care Unit, the use of more than 60% oxygen for more than four hours is avoided if possible.

SUMMARY AND RECOMMENDATIONS

The provision of adequate oxygen to the cells is the primary aim of the management of the critically ill in the ITU. Achieving this requires a rational approach to therapy which itself requires a thorough understanding of how oxygen normally reaches the cells (Fig 2.6) and effective monitoring of this process.

The equipment required includes a blood gas analyser and oximeter (see Chapter 5). The precise method of presenting the data has not been standardised or agreed upon. In presenting the data, it is important to distinguish between the measured and derived values because even a small error in measurement or its documentation may be magnified in the derived values (Table 2.7). This may then result in inappropriate interpretation and management of the patient. A comprehensive understanding of the physiology and pathology of oxygenation remains the single most important factor in managing the critically ill.

FLUID AND ELECTROLYTES

FLUID COMPARTMENTS

The body is composed of approximately 70% water, the appropriate distribution of which is fundamental to cellular function. However, water homeostasis cannot be considered in isolation since the distribution of water between the vascular, interstitial and intracellular compartments depends on the solute content of each compartment. Although the osmolality of the intracellular and extracellular fluid is the same, there are marked differences in solute content, including dissolved ions such as sodium, chloride, potassium, and macromolecules such as proteins and aminoglycan polymers. The distribution of dissolved ions between different body compartments, frequently with enormous concentration gradients across semipermeable membranes, are maintained by energy-consuming ion pumps.

Simplification of the body's fluid-holding compartments into vascular, interstitial and intracellular, allows some comparison to be made of the relative concentrations of dissolved solutes, and how they change during shock.

The interstitial space is approximately four times larger than the vascular space. Organ for organ, the skin and viscera have the highest interstitial volumes, but because of its overall mass, skeletal muscle includes between 25 and 40% of the total body interstitial volume. Within the interstitial space, two phases can be identified. One is a polymeric matrix of glycosaminoglycans which traps water and excludes protein partly because of the latter's size, and also because the matrix is negatively charged. The other is a free fluid phase which contains water, proteins and dissolved ions. The capillary endothelium is not completely impermeable to plasma proteins, and the protein content of interstitial fluid is about 30% that of plasma, and contains about two thirds of all the albumin within the body. Plasma proteins reaching the interstitium are returned to the systemic vascular circulation via the lymphatic drainage system. The major reason for the difference in electrolyte concentrations between plasma and interstitial fluid (see Table 2.9) is the negative charge on glycosaminoglycans, and Donnan forces set up because of the differing protein concentrations.

In 1896 Starling described the pressure-dependent exchange of fluids between the capillaries and the interstitial space. Typical values for the forces which drive fluid from the arterial end of the capillary are:

Outward Pressures

Capillary Pressure (derived from the pumping action of the heart)	30 mmHg
Negative interstitial free fluid (derived from the lymphatic drainage drawing fluid from the interstitium)	3 mmHg
Interstitial fluid colloidal osmotic pressure	8 mmHg
Total outward infiltrate pressure	41 mmHg

Inward Pressures

Plasma colloidal osmotic pressure	28 mmHg

Net outward filtration pressure (41-28) = 13 mmHg

At the venous end of the capillary there is a net fluid absorption driven by the plasma colloidal osmotic pressure which supervenes over the reduced capillary pressure:

Outward Pressures

Capillary pressure (reduced because of the capillary resistance)	10 mmHg
Negative interstitial free fluid pressure	3 mmHg

Interstitial fluid colloidal osmotic pressure	8 mmHg
Total outward infiltrate pressure	21 mmHg

Inward Pressures

Plasma colloidal osmotic pressure	28 mmHg

Net inward filtration pressure (28-21) = 7 mmHg

Despite the apparent discrepancy between the net outward filtration pressure at the arterial end of the capillary (13 mmHg) and the net inward filtration pressure (only 7 mmHg) at the venous end of the capillary, there is a steady state of filtration and reabsorption. This is for two reasons. Firstly, there are more capillaries towards the venous end of the vascular bed than arteriolar capillaries, the former present a larger surface area for reabsorption back into the circulation albeit at lower pressures. Secondly, about 10% of fluid filtered from the arterial end of the capillaries is drained by the lymphatic system.

It might be anticipated on theoretical grounds that patients with increased blood pressure would develop oedema. However, essential hypertension is due to arterial (i.e., precapillary) vasoconstriction, with normal capillary perfusion pressures, except in specialised capillary beds such as the retina where hypertension does cause oedema.

Thus under normal circumstances, the systemic microcirculation maintains a free flow of fluid between the vascular and interstitial spaces. An understanding of these forces helps to explain the interstitial oedema which accompanies heart failure. Sudden heart failure does not cause immediate peripheral oedema, because as arterial pressure falls there is a rise in right atrial venous pressure, but as the cardiac output continues to fall, the arterial and venous pressures equilibrate at about 13 mmHg. However, reduced cardiac output, leading to reduced renal perfusion accompanied by a fall in glomerular filtration, stimulates the release of renin and hence angiotensin II which causes rapid vasoconstriction, and increased aldosterone secretion. After about 24 hours, the rise in circulating aldosterone concentration leads to sodium retention with accompanying water retention, increasing venous filling pressure and restoring cardiac output towards normal. The increased venous pressure with normal arterial pressure prevents the return of filtered fluid at the venous end of the capillaries where plasma colloidal osmotic pressure, which would normally force fluid back into the circulation, is overwhelmed by the increased venous pressure. Oedema can also be caused by a shift of plasma proteins from the vascular to interstitial space. This occurs when there is an increase in vascular permeability to macromolecules due to the inflammatory response seen, for example, in septicaemia, severe pancreatitis or major trauma. Table 2.8 summarises the principal mechanisms of oedema formation.

Table 2.8 Principal causes and mechanisms of tissue oedema.

Causes	Mechanism
• Heart failure	Increased venous pressure due to renin/aldosterone-driven fluid retention overwhelms plasma colloidal osmotic pressure which would normally drive fluid back into venous capillaries
• Venous outflow blockage	Increased venous pressure which overcomes plasma colloidal onocotic pressure
• Increased capillary permeability	Increased movement of plasma proteins into the interstitial space reduces plasma colloidal oncotic pressure and increases interstitial fluid oncotic pressure driving fluid from plasma into the interstitual space

Moving from the interstitium to the cytoplasm, the most striking differences are concentrations of sodium and potassium, with potassium replacing sodium as the major intracellular cation (Table 2.9). Since these large concentration gradients are maintained across the cytoplasmic membrane, which is semipermeable, a constant energy-consuming transport of sodium out of the cell and potassium into the cell is required. Cleavage of one molecule at ATP to ADP and the liberation of a high energy phosphate group produces a conformational change in a carrier protein for sodium and potassium, which extrudes three molecules of sodium from within the cell and transfers two molecules of potassium into the cell. By constantly pumping sodium out of the cell, osmotic forces produce an associated loss of water from within the cell. Thus the sodium/potassium pump controls the intracellular fluid volume. When there is a shortage of ATP, the cell will tend to swell due to reduced sodium extrusion and associated water retention. For this reason, the extracellular sodium concentration will tend to fall, and potassium concentration rise. The net removal of three sodium ions for an intake of two potassium ions creates a membrane potential with an intracellular negative charge.

Table 2.9 Approximately concentrations of the electrolytes/ solutes in body compartments.

SOLUTE	COMPARTMENT		
	Vascular	Interstitial	Intracellular
Sodium (mmol/L)	143	140	12
Potassium (mmol/L)	4.2	4.0	150
Calcium (mmol/L)	2.4	1.3	2×10^{-4}
Magnesium (mmol/L)	0.95	0.90	20
Chloride (mmol/L)	95	87	4
Phosphate (mmol/L)	1.2	1.1	11
Bicarbonate (mmol/L)	24	24	10
Protein (g/L)	70	20	250

Another feature of the cytoplasm is its extremely low calcium concentration. Calcium shifts between intracellular organelles and the cytoplasm form an important intracellular, and possibly intercellular, second messenger pathway for metabolic control.

FLUID AND ELECTROLYTE HOMEOSTASIS IN SHOCK

Dietary sodium intake is in the region of 100-150 mmol/24h, which is mostly excreted in the urine with small amounts in sweat and faeces. It is difficult to define a normal daily requirement for sodium in man since in a steady state, input will equal output. For electrolytes such as sodium and potassium, balance is maintained by the kidney in the face of large variations in both intake and losses. The faecal and sweat sodium losses become significant in diarrhoeal illnesses and in profuse sweating. Severe dietary sodium restriction can reduce urinary sodium to almost zero. Water and sodium homeostasis move in directions required to maintain normal plasma osmolality and an adequate circulating blood volume. Redistribution of fluid between compartments, or changes in osmolality lead to compensatory changes. A sudden reduction in available blood to fill the vascular tree as a result of massive blood loss or redistribution of blood into an expanded capillary bed volume as occurs in septic shock, results in reduced cardiac filling pressure and a reduction in cardiac output.

ACUTE COMPENSATION

Blood pressure is protected by rapid release of adrenaline and noradrenaline leading to arteriolar vasoconstriction in the skin, splanchnic bed, and skeletal muscles. In shock, reduced renal perfusion, reduced sodium delivery to the kidney and increased sympathetic beta-adrenergic activity all stimulate release of renin from the juxtaglomerular cells, which acts on circulating angiotensinogen to produce the decapeptide angiotensin I. Angiotensin I is converted to angiotensin II, an octapeptide, by the action of converting enzyme in the capillary beds of the lungs and other tissues. Angiotensin II is a potent vasoconstrictor, augments the pressor actions of catecholamines, and helps to maintain

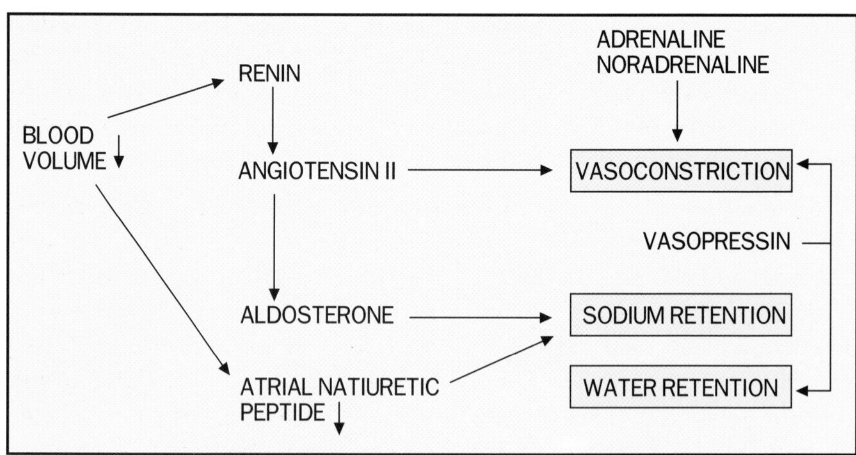

Fig 2.7 Principal endocrine pathways for maintenance of blood pressure and blood volume in shock.

blood pressure in shock. In acute shock, the posterior pituitary releases vasopressin which increases renal tubular permeability to water helping to restore the reduced blood volume. Vasopressin also acts as a vasoconstrictor (Fig 2.7).

As capillary perfusion pressure falls, pre-capillary vasoconstriction is mediated by angiotensin II and catecholamines. Pre-capillary vasoconstriction leads to arterio-venous shunting, where arteriolar blood 'bypasses' the capillaries, and returns to the venous circulation. Tissue ischaemia ensues which causes capillary vasodilatation and an increase in the vascular bed volume (Fig 2.1).

Although these rapid responses may restore blood pressure, normal blood flow cannot be restored to the tissues until an adequate blood volume is restored. Following severe vasoconstriction, in the absence of any external resuscitation, the capillary pressure derived from the pumping action of the heart is reduced. This creates a net inward pressure within the capillaries, derived from the plasma colloidal osmotic pressure, driving fluid from the interstitium (and ultimately from the cells across an osmotic gradient) into the capillaries. Thus, in early shock, blood haemoglobin and haemocrit values may be normal, but as compensatory fluid shifts take place over the subsequent 2 to 6 hours, haemoglobin concentration and haematocrit values fall. However if the hypovolaemia is severe and compensatory mechanisms are inadequate, then a decompensated state ensues, when vasoconstriction can no longer be maintained and arteriolar resistance falls, large volumes of plasma start to leak from capillaries and an irreversible state of shock develops. It is avoidance of these terminal events that is the aim of intensive resuscitation regimes.

The events described above are rapid responses to an acute deficiency of the blood volume available to fill the vascular tree. The blood supply to essential organs is preserved by selective arteriolar vasoconstriction, with hypoperfusion of certain tissues such as skin. For example, angiotensin II also stimulates the local release of vasodilatory prostaglandins within the kidney to maintain renal blood flow, despite profound vasoconstriction elsewhere. For this reason, nonsteroidal anti-inflammatory drugs which inhibit cyclooxygenase and reduce local prostaglandin production, can produce a profound reduction in glomerular filtration in patients who are hypovolaemia and whose circulation is maintained by high concentrations of angiotensin II.

Within a few hours, the blood volume is augmented by fluid shifts from the intracellular space. Longer term compensatory mechanisms then come into play which appear to be directed to a more permanent correction of the acute fluid and electrolyte derangement following shock.

LONGER TERM COMPENSATION

Angiotensin II stimulates the zona glomerulosa of the adrenal gland to release aldosterone which promotes reabsorption of sodium and excretion of potassium from the renal tubule and the gut. Angiotensin II also stimulates pituitary release of ACTH and vasopressin. The effects of ACTH will be discussed later. In shock, vasopressin from the posterior pituitary supports the immediate vasoconstricting pressor response and increases the permeability to water of the distal convoluted tubule and collecting ducts of the kidney causing water retention. Release of atrial natiuretic peptide (ANP) from cells in the aortic arch is influenced by changes in blood volume. In patients with reduced blood volume, such as following burn injury, admission ANP concentrations are low thus promoting sodium retention. Values rise progressively after three days post burn to supranormal concentrations which coincides with a naturesis.

CARBOHYDRATE

Both in normal metabolism and in shock, energy is provided by oxidation of carbohydrate, protein and lipid derived either from the diet or body stores. Although carbohydrate, in the form of glycogen, represents less than one per cent of the body's total energy reserves, it is a crucial substrate for the central nervous system and for short bursts of intense muscular activity. The brain can adapt to using either glucose or ketones as substrate.

Approximately 25% of glycogen reserves are in the liver, the remainder being stored in skeletal muscle. During fasting the liver plays a key role in the maintenance of normal blood glucose concentrations. Hepatic glycogen phosphorylase and glucose 6-phosphatase allow glucose to be mobilised from glycogen and released into circulation, providing an

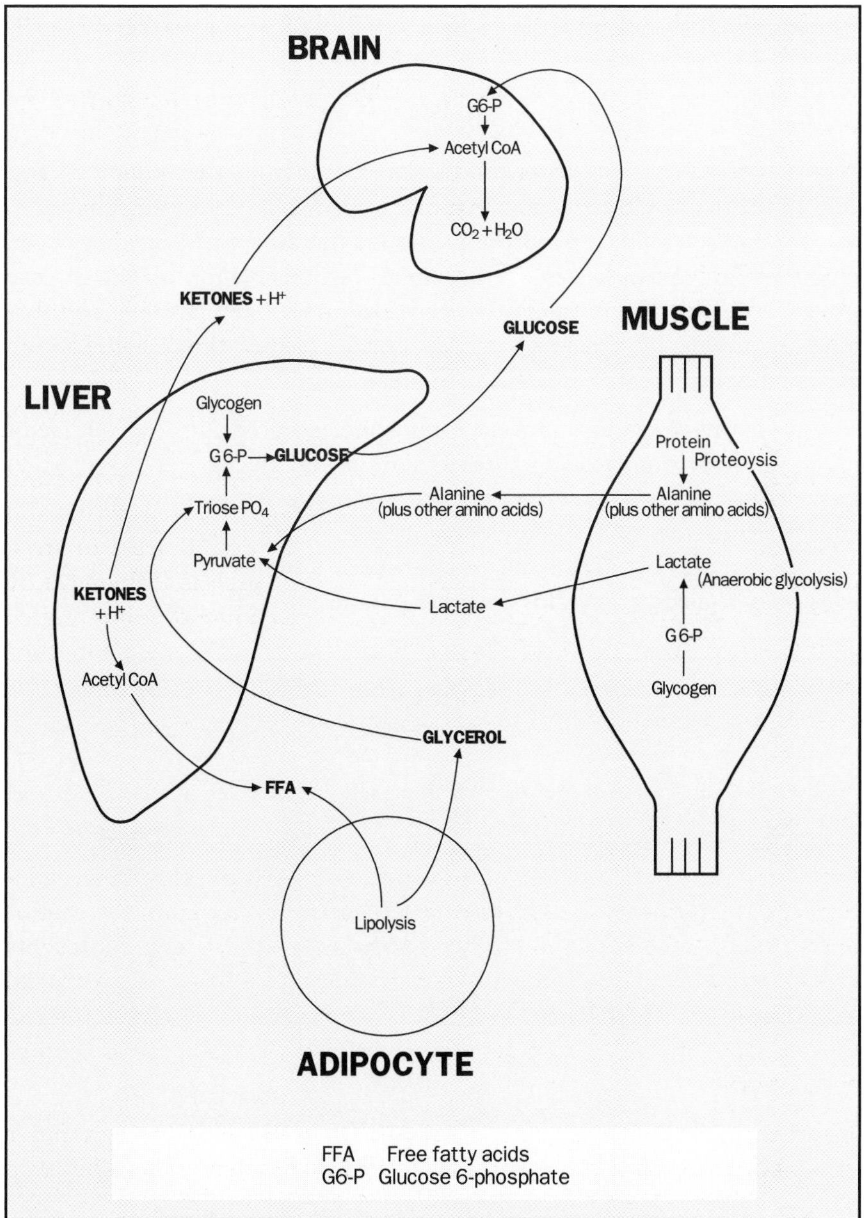

Fig 2.8 Glucose homeostasis in shock. A summary of the pathways which maintain supply of glucose and ketones in shock.

energy substrate for distant organs. When hepatic glycogen stores are replete they will maintain normal blood glucose concentrations for up to 24 hours, but in the hypermetabolic state of shock, glycogen stores become depleted much more quickly.

About 80% of hepatic glucose production comes from glycogenolysis and 20% from gluconeogenesis of which half is from lactate and the remainder from amino acids (Fig 2.8). During fasting, once all the glycogen has been mobilised, gluconeogenesis alone becomes responsible for hepatic glucose production. The fasting pool of glucose within the circulation is approximately equivalent to the hourly hepatic glucose output, thus hepatic failure can rapidly lead to life threatening hypoglycaemia.

In muscle the absence of glucose 6-phosphatase precludes the release of glycogen-derived glucose into the circulation, and glycogen is converted to glucose-6-phosphate which enters the glycolytic pathway to meet local energy requirements. The conversion of 1 mole of glucose to 2 of pyruvate, releases 2 moles of ATP, whilst oxidation of 2 moles of pyruvate in the tricarboxylic acid cycle yields a further 6 moles of ATP.

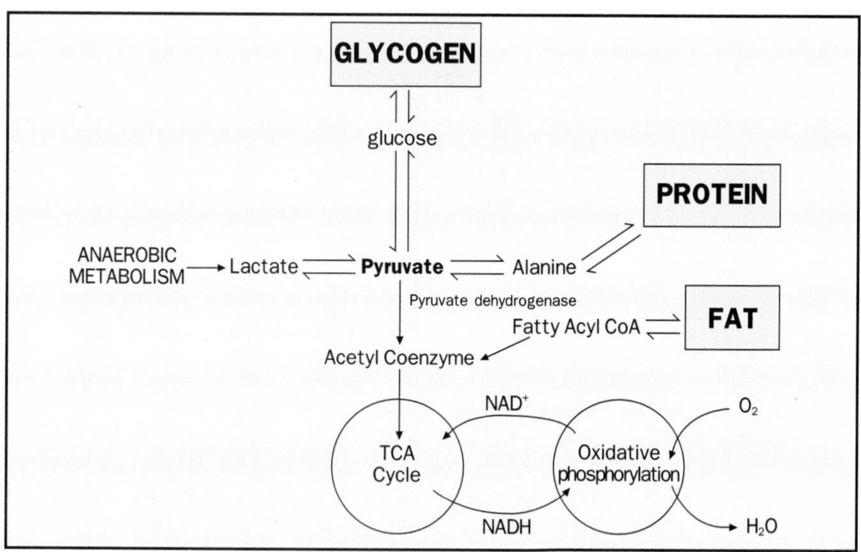

Fig 2.9 Intermediary metabolism in shock. Lipogenesis and glucogenesis are not simple reversals of these pathways.

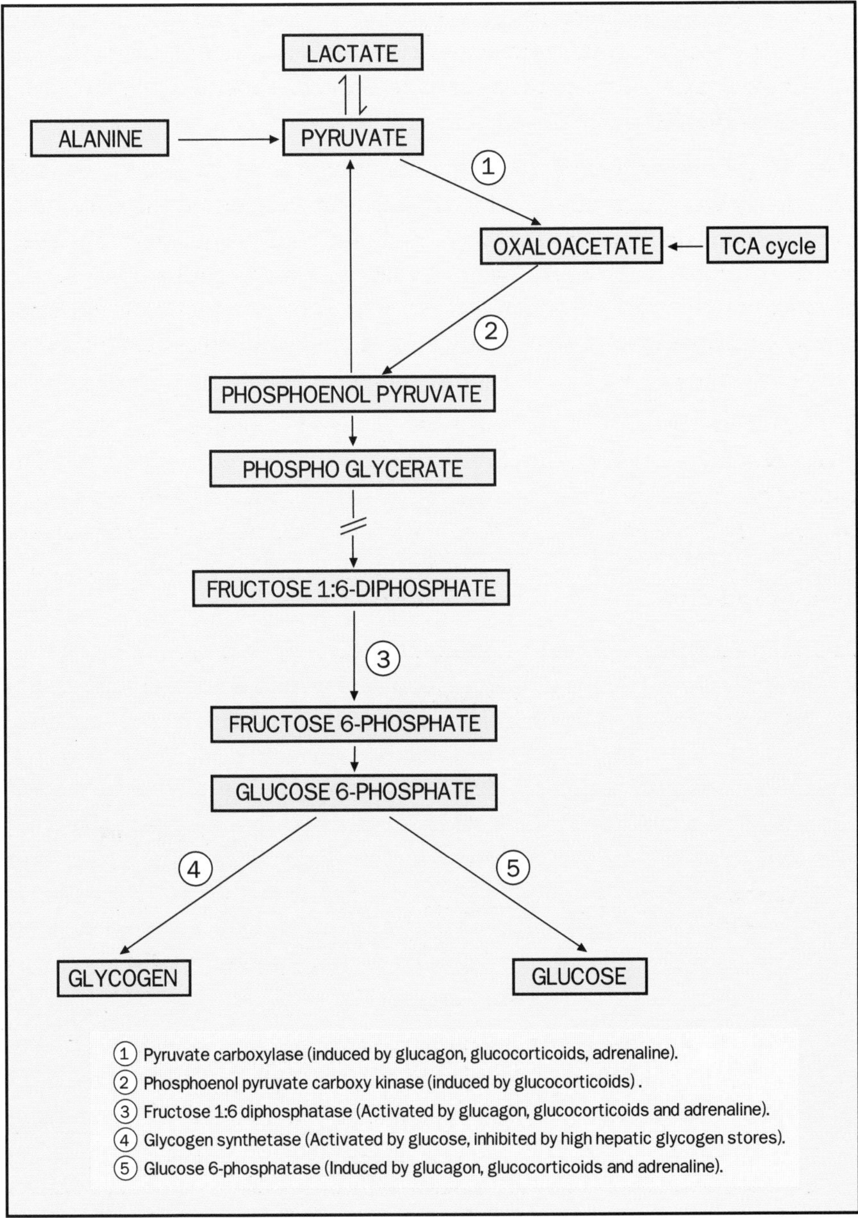

Fig 2.10 Control of gluconeogenesis.

Oxidation of pyruvate to acetyl coenzyme A is catalysed by the enzyme pyruvate dehydrogenase, which depends upon a suitable electron acceptor, NAD^+. Entry of pyruvate-derived acetyl CoA into the tricarboxylic acid cycle forms a critical balance point between aerobic and anaerobic metabolism of carbohydrate (Fig 2.9).

The tricarboxylic acid cycle is a series of dehydrogenation and decarboxylation reactions that convert a molecule of acetyl CoA to CoA, carbon dioxide and water. The dehydrogenation reactions within the cycle, whereby an electron and its associated proton are removed from the substrate, require a suitable electron acceptor such as NAD^+, which undergoes reduction to NADH. Mitochondrial oxidation of NADH back to NAD^+ requires an adequate supply of oxygen.

GLUCOSE METABOLISM IN SHOCK

In the shocked patient, blood glucose concentration is increased due to gluconeogenesis from substrates derived from anaerobic metabolism and proteolysis: pathways that are facilitated by increased concentrations of catecholamines, cortisol, growth hormone and glucagon (Fig 2.10). This occurs despite the depletion of glycogen stores and normal or increased concentrations of insulin. Glucose uptake by cells is increased, but glucose oxidation is not. This is the result of reduced activity of both pyruvate dehydrogenase and the tricarboxylic acid cycle, both of which are limited by the shortage of NAD^+. Compounds such as pyruvate, alanine and lactate accumulate and are returned to the liver where they are utilised as substrates for gluconeogenesis. In this way the liver and to some extent the kidney, provide a supply of glucose for glucose dependent tissues such as the central and peripheral nervous system, leukocytes, red blood cells, bone marrow, renal medulla, gut and healing wounds.

The reduced delivery of oxygen to the tissues in shock limits mitochondrial oxidation of NADH to NAD^+. The NAD^+/NADH ratio falls, slowing the tricarboxylic acid cycle and causing acetyl coenzyme A concentrations to rise. In shock, the accumulation of acetyl coenzyme A, an allosteric inhibitor of pyruvate dehydrogenase, leads to a fall in the activity of this enzyme. A shortage of NAD^+ to act as an electron acceptor is also a limiting factor. Pyruvate concentrations increase both because of the inhibition of pyruvate dehydrogenase and because of pyruvate generation from alanine released during proteolysis. This latter process accounts for up to 75% of the increase in circulating pyruvate in shocked patients. Pyruvate concentrations also rise because of an increase in glycolysis. Glycolysis is regulated by the activity of phosphofructokinase, which is activated by low concentrations of ATP. Thus in shock, more glucose or glucose 6-phosphate is driven through the glycolytic pathway to pyruvate (Fig 2.9).

Pyruvate reduction to lactate by lactate dehydrogenase, reoxidises NADH to NAD^+, which is of value in a hypoxic state, where aerobic oxidation of NADH via oxygen-dependent mitochondrial electron transfer is limited. Anaerobic metabolism can continue until toxic concentrations of lactate develop. The ratio of lactate to pyruvate and that of β-hydroxybutyrate to acetoacetate reflect the NAD^+/NADH ratio, and ultimately reflect tissue oxygenation.

PROTEIN

Protein turnover is normally a balance between proteolysis and the synthesis of new protein, the net result being the maintenance of muscle mass, visceral protein and plasma protein concentrations. In shock, there is a profound alteration in protein metabolism, with skeletal muscle proteolysis and amino acid shuttling from muscle to the liver and gut, providing substrates for gluconeogenesis and the tricarboxylic acid cycle.

PROTEOLYSIS

The negative nitrogen balance seen in patients with shock is due to the breakdown of skeletal muscle proteins. Only about 30% of the body's protein is readily available as a source of energy, further proteolysis results in life-threatening damage to essential structural and secreted proteins. In shock, free amino acid concentrations in muscle cells rise, and amino acids such as alanine and glutamine are released into the circulation at 3 to 5 times the normal rate. Only about 20% of amino acids released from muscle are used for local energy production via gluconeogensis to glucose 6-phosphate, the rest are transported to the liver for gluconeogenesis and protein synthesis (Fig 2.11).

In the early post-sepsis or trauma period, amino acid utilisation is sluggish and blood concentrations tend to be high, but during the subsequent hypermetabolic stage there is increased hepatic clearance of amino acids

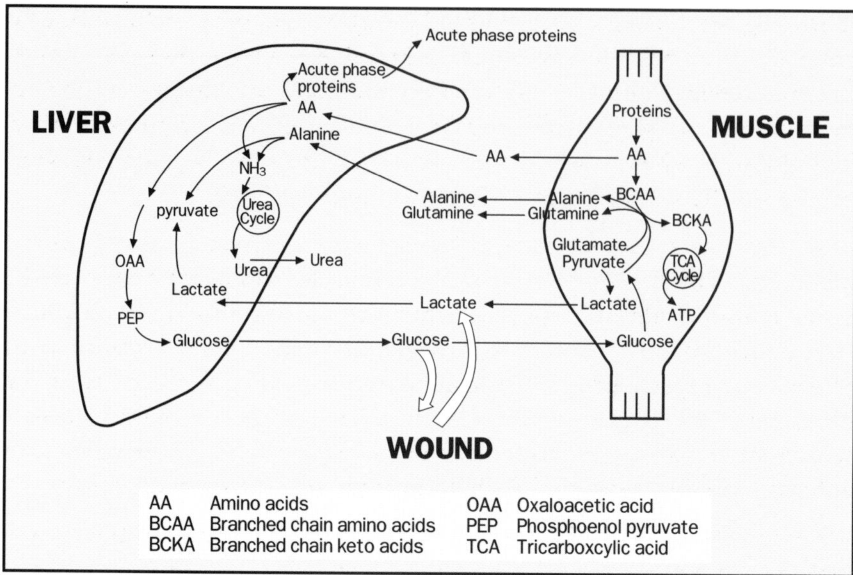

Fig 2.11 Protein metabolism in the critically ill. In shock skeletal muscle proteolysis releases amino acids providing substrates for gluconeogenesis and the tricarboxylic acid cycle (TCA) in the liver and gut.

and despite their increased mobilisation from muscle, blood concentrations tend to be below normal. However if liver function deteriorates, concentrations rise, especially those of aromatic amino acids. Circulating alanine can be extracted by the liver and deaminated to form ammonia and pyruvate. The former enters the urea cycle and the latter is utilised in gluconeogensis. In liver failure the blood concentrations of ammonia rise and those of urea fall. Urea is the major contributor to the increased urinary nitrogen losses seen in critically ill patients as a result of proteolysis.

Circulating glutamine can be trapped by the kidney and intestine. In the kidney the deamination of glutamine releases ammonium ions and glutamate. From an acid-base perspective, renal excretion of nitrogen in the form of ammonium has an advantage over hepatic ureagenesis, since the latter generates hydrogen ions while the former provides additional route for hydrogen ion excretion. Glutamate can be further metabolised to α-oxoglutarate which can be used for gluconeogensis in the kidney or enter the tricarboxylic acid cycle. Glutamine seems to be important for the maintenance of intestinal function and mucosal integrity. In the gut, metabolism of glutamine and pyruvate releases ammonia, alpha ketoglutarate which enters the tricarboxylic acid cycle, and alanine which can be shuttled to the liver for gluconeogenesis (Fig 2.11).

Branched chain amino acids (leucine, isoleucine and valine) are not metabolised by the liver but by skeletal muscle, and may be converted to other amino acids, incorporated into the muscle proteins and play a regulatory role in protein synthesis. Branched chain amino acids released by muscle proteolysis can be transaminated with pyruvate and glutamate to form alanine and glutamine and branched chain keto acids which, after further metabolism via propionyl CoA to succinyl CoA, enter the tricarboxylic acid cycle to provide the muscle with energy.

Whilst in starvation, administration of adequate calories in the form of carbohydrate or lipid will stop muscle wasting proteolysis in septic or trauma patients cannot be suppressed by normal or even supra normal amounts of carbohydrate. This seems to be because the principal stimulation for protein breakdown is the secretion of cytokines from activated macrophages.

ACUTE PHASE PROTEIN SYNTHESIS

The synthesis of acute phase proteins by the liver is stimulated by cytokines such as tumour necrosis factor and interleukins 1 and 6 in conjunction with increased concentrations of cortisol and glucagon. The acute phase proteins include fibrinogen, which is essential for haemostasis, $alpha_2$-macroglobulin and $alpha_1$-antitrypsin which inhibit the systemic effects of proteases released from inflammatory cells, caeruloplasmin, a free radical scavenger and C-reactive protein which is involved in bacterial opsonisation, complement activation and phagocytosis.

In addition to stimulating hepatic acute phase protein synthesis, tumour necrosis factor and interleukin-1 suppress albumin synthesis. This 'reprioritization' is probably important because albumin synthesis normally uses up a large part of the amino acid pool, which in shock would be needed for synthesis of essential proteins for host defence, wound healing and the acute phase reactants.

LIPIDS

Oxidation of fat stores provides a longer term energy supply for the fasting patient. Comparison of the available energy per gram dry weight reveals that carbohydrate and protein each produce about 4 kcals/gram while fat produces 9 kcals/gram. Thus, in terms of storage efficiency, body fat provides a better and longer term energy source in the fasting patient.

However, with the exception of glycerol released from triglycerides, carbon skeletons derived from lipids are not used for glucose synthesis, thus proteins form the main source of carbon for gluconeogenesis.

Under normal conditions fatty acids are mobilised from fat stores by the action of increased concentrations of cortisol, catecholamines and glucagon, and in response to low insulin concentrations. The free fatty acids are transported bound to plasma albumin. Fatty acids enter the cell and are complexed with coenzyme A to form fatty acyl coenzyme A, and in this form they enter the mitochondria facilitated by a carnitine-dependent mechanism. Beta oxidation of fatty acids produces ketones,

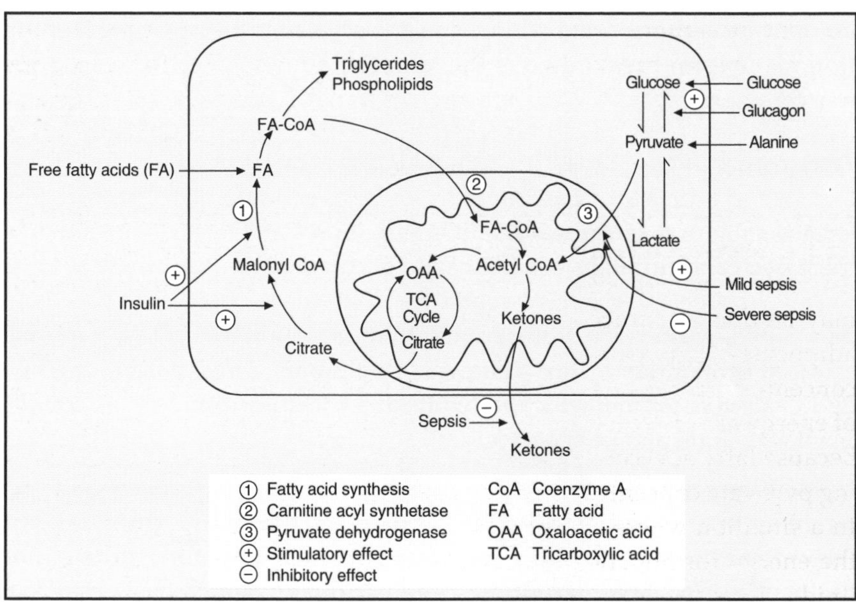

Fig 2.12 Lipid metabolism in the critically ill. Lipolysis is increased in response to cortisol, glucagon and catecholamines, with the release of free fatty acids.

(acetoacetate and β-hydroxybutyrate) which are exported as an energy source, and acetyl coenzyme A which enters the tricarboxylic acid cycle. Increased citrate concentration leads to a rise in malonyl coenzyme A in the cytoplasm, which inhibits the carnitine-dependent fatty acid entry into the mitochondria, thereby providing a feedback control mechanism for mitochondrial fatty acid oxidation (Fig 2.12).

Starvation or diabetic ketoacidosis is associated with increased fatty acid mobilisation, and oxidation of free fatty acids to acetyl coenzyme A, which is further cleaved to release ketones. The rise in acetoacetate leads to acidaemia. The lack of insulin in diabetic ketoacidosis, reduced cytoplasmic malonyl coenzyme A production and *de novo* lipid synthesis, accelerate mitochondrial entry of fatty acids, fatty acid oxidation and ketogenesis.

In critically ill septic patients, free fatty acid and glycerol production increases due to increased lipolysis in response to cortisol, catecholamines and glucagon. Mobilised free fatty acids are oxidised to provide energy and ketones or reincorporated into triglycerides. However, ketogenesis is not so pronounced as in diabetic ketoacidosis, probably because of the normal or high circulating insulin concentrations. Insulin promotes malonyl coenzyme A and fatty acid synthesis. Malonyl coenzyme A inhibits fatty acyl coenzyme A entry into mitochondria, thereby limiting fatty acid oxidation and ketone formation.

In spite of the increase in lipid degradation in the critically ill, free fatty acid concentrations in plasma are generally normal but triglyceride concentrations are sharply increased. Impaired triglyceride removal may be due to reduced lipoprotein lipase activity in muscle cells and adipocytes. It appears that although intracellular fatty acyl coenzyme A concentrations are increased in shock, as are ketone bodies, other sources of energy are provided by proteolysis and gluconeogenesis. This may be because fatty acyl coenzyme A inhibits pyruvate dehydrogenase, allowing pyruvate concentrations to rise and thus promoting gluconeogenesis. In a situation where energy from glucose oxidation is in short supply, the energy for hepatic gluconeogensis is provided by the oxidation of lipids. Thus lipids appear to provide energy for gluconeogensis, and inhibit the entry of pyruvate and other glucose precursors into the tricarboxylic acid cycle. The development of hepatic steatosis in the critically ill may be explained by the high concentrations of fatty acids within the cytoplasm inhibiting fatty acid entry into mitochondria where beta oxidation could take place, and promoting triglyceride synthesis and hepatic fat storage.

SUMMARY OF CARBOHYDRATE, PROTEIN AND LIPID METABOLISM IN THE CRITICALLY ILL

Patients requiring intensive care are frequently starved, with depleted glycogen stores, yet have increased energy requirements.

In most patients fat stores will still be intact, but lipid, (with the exception of glycerol derived from triglycerides) cannot provide the carbon skeleton for glucose synthesis. Protein from skeletal muscle is degraded to alanine, lactate and pyruvate, which are used for gluconeogenesis and acute phase protein synthesis. Synthesis of some proteins such as albumin is suppressed. Branched chain amino acids are largely used for local muscle energy needs.

Fatty acids provide energy for these processes, inhibit glucose oxidation and shunt substrates such as pyruvate towards gluconeogenesis.

Cortisol, glucagon, catecholamines and growth hormone facilitate these processes (Table 2.10) together with inflammatory cytokines (Table 2.11 and Fig 2.13). These cytokines are secreted by activated macrophages found in sites of inflammation (infection, trauma, surgery etc). Their effects may be intracellular (autocrine) or localised (paracrine); however measurable amounts have been found in the circulation in severe inflammatory conditions suggesting that they may also act as hormones (endocrine).

NUTRITIONAL SUPPORT

INTRODUCTION

Considerable amounts of some nutrients are stored in the body. Even lean individuals have fat stores sufficient to provide most of the body's normal energy requirements for several weeks. Stores of carbohydrate (mainly hepatic glycogen) are limited and become depleted within 24 hours of fasting after which obligatory requirements for glucose, although decreased by adaptive processes, must be met by gluconeogenesis. There are no true stores of protein in the body, and

Table 2.10 Principal mediators of metabolic changes associated with shock.

Proteolysis increased by
- Cortisol
- Glucagon
- IL-1
- PAF

(TNF, IL-1 and IL-6 inhibit hepatic albumin synthesis)

Lipolysis increased by
- Cortisol
- Glucagon
- Catecholamines
- Growth hormone

(TNF inhibits lipoprotein lipase)

Gluconeogenesis increased by
- Cortisol
- Glucagon
- Growth hormone (liver only)

Glycogenolysis increased by
- Glucagon
- Catecholamines
- Cortisol (muscle only)

Hepatic Acute Phase Protein Synthesis increased by
- Cortisol
- IL-6
- IL-1
- TNF

IL-1 Interleukin 1
IL-6 Interleukin 6
PAF Platelet activating factor
TNF Tumour necrosis factor

(N.B. Insulin opposes lipolysis, proteolysis and glycogenolysis)

Table 2.11 Metabolic effects of inflammatory cytokines in shock.

TUMOUR NECROSIS FACTOR (increased)
- Increases plasma triglycerides
- Decreases hepatic albumin synthesis

INTERLEUKINS 1 & 6 (increased)
- Increase oxygen consumption
- Increase basal metabolic rate
- Increase hepatic amino acid sequestration
- Increase hepatic zinc and iron sequestration
- Increase skeletal muscle proteolysis
- Increase hepatic acute phase protein synthesis
- Decrease hepatic albumin synthesis
- Stimulate pancreatic glucagon and insulin release

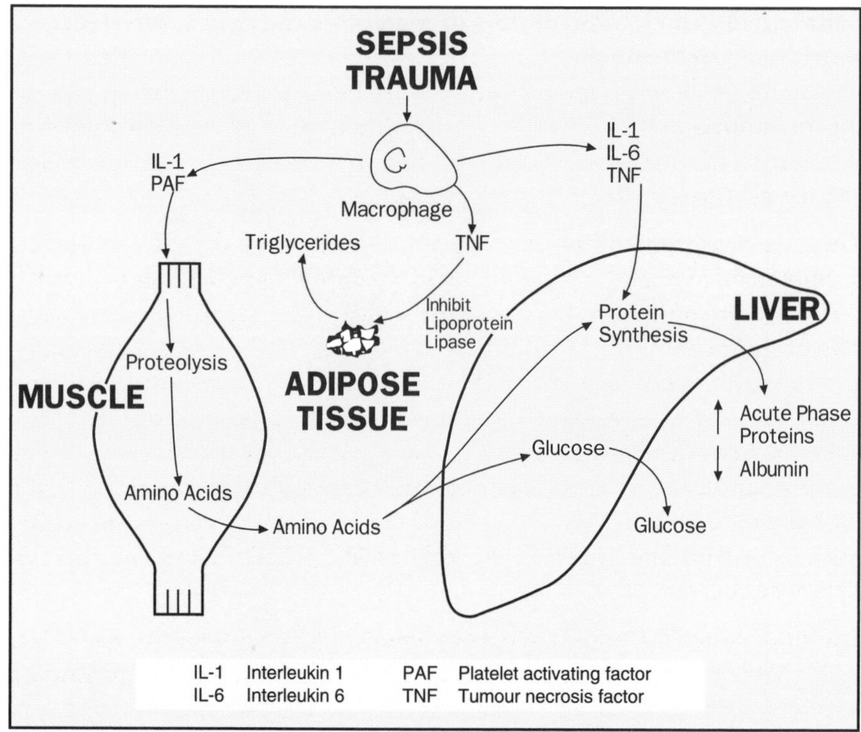

Fig 2.13 The effects of cytokines on protein and fat.

during fasting, requirements for essential protein synthesis must be met by the degradation of other (e.g., muscle) protein, the process which also supports gluconeogenesis. Body stores of minerals and vitamins vary between being sufficient to supply requirements for months (e.g. vitamin A, vitamin B_{12}), and for only a few weeks (e.g., thiamine, zinc).

In normal individuals, nutrient requirements are met by eating food but there is little evidence that short periods of starvation do any organic harm. The same is true of previously adequately nourished patients admitted to an ITU during the immediate (e.g., 24 hours) post-operative period following uncomplicated major surgery not involving the gut (e.g., open heart surgery), and in whom there is a high probability of an early resumption of normal eating.

However, for many patients admitted to ITUs, this probability is low, and nutritional support will be required. Some of these patients are malnourished on admission and have an obvious requirement for early nutritional support. Nevertheless, the majority of ITU patients are reasonably well nourished on admission, but are at high risk of becoming malnourished as a result of a combination of decreased intake of nutrients, increased losses (e.g., through fistulae) and increased requirements (e.g., due to trauma or sepsis).

There is no dispute that, if the gut is working, it should be used to supply nutrients. Not only does enteral feeding allow nutrients to enter the bloodstream by the normal route, so that they are (with the exception of short chain triacylglycerols) first presented to the liver, the major site of nutrient processing, there is increasing evidence that the enterocytes of the small intestine rely to some extent on luminal nutrients for their nutrition. If the gut is not used, its motility decreases but, more importantly, villous atrophy and enterocyte dysfunction impair its barrier function. This increases the risk of translocation of microorganisms from the lumen of the gut into the bloodstream and thus the risk of septicaemia.

The rule in the ITU, as elsewhere, should be, 'If the gut works, use it.' If, as is usually the case, eating is impossible, continuous nasogastric or nasojejunal feeding using one of the many commercially available feeds may be feasible. Subsequent enteral feeding is greatly facilitated if a nasojejunal tube is placed during the course of abdominal surgery. If artificial enteral feeding is required in the long term, consideration should be given to the provision of a gastrostomy. The endoscopically-guided, percutaneous procedure is simple, safe, and well-tolerated.

If patients have intestinal failure, it will be necessary to consider parenteral (intravenous) feeding. Intestinal failure can be defined as a disorder of the gut in which its ability to process and absorb nutrients is less than is required for the maintenance of adequate nutrition. Frequent indications for parenteral feeding in patients in ITU include prolonged ileus (e.g., because of sepsis or the use of muscle paralyzing drugs to facilitate mechanical ventilation) and acute pancreatitis and its complications.

The principles and practice of providing nutritional support, both enteral and parenteral, are well covered in several textbooks and reviews (see 'Further Reading') and will only be summarized here although certain noteworthy points will be emphasized. The regimen provided must take account of the patient's requirements, and be administered by an appropriate route. Rigorous care of delivery systems is necessary to prevent mechanical complications and infection. Careful clinical and laboratory monitoring is necessary to assess the efficacy of nutritional support and to minimize the risk of metabolic complications.

There is considerable evidence to indicate that the efficacy and safety of artificial nutritional support is improved if it is provided under the supervision of a multidisciplinary nutrition support team. The exact composition of such teams will depend on local factors but most will include a nurse specialist, dietitian, pharmacist, clinical biochemist and a clinical specialist - physician, surgeon or anaesthetist. All have important and complementary roles. The clinical biochemist will be particularly concerned with the assessment of laboratory parameters of nutritional status, and laboratory monitoring for metabolic complications.

The nutritional pathophysiology of the ITU patient has been discussed above and the provision of nutritional support must reflect this. But attainment of the ultimate goal of nutritional support - the restoration and maintenance of adequate nutrition - may be compromised by the severity of the underlying illness and its associated metabolic response.

NUTRITIONAL ASSESSMENT AND THE COMPONENTS OF PARENTERAL FEEDS

Numerous algorithms have been devised to assess nutritional status. These include various laboratory, anthropometric and functional tests, both alone and in weighted combinations in so-called 'nutritional indices'. While these methods may provide a baseline for the assessment of response to the provision of nutritional support, none is reliably superior to experienced clinical assessment in identifying the need to initiate such support.

Energy

Objective assessment of requirements can provide valuable information. It has long been considered that the energy expenditure of severely ill patients can be up to 50% higher than normal basal requirements, but measurements made using indirect calorimetry have indicated that this is not usually the case, and that the average expenditure is often not more than 10% greater than the resting energy expenditure in health, that is, approximately 30kcal/kg/24h. Massively increased energy expenditure is confined largely to patients with severe burns or major trauma and there is little evidence that the provision of energy at a rate to match expenditure reverses the underlying catabolic processes in such cases.

Indirect calorimetry involves measurement of oxygen consumption and carbon dioxide production and permits the calculation of the respiratory quotient (RQ, CO_2 production/O_2 consumption). The RQ provides information on substrate utilization. When energy is being derived from fat, the RQ is 0.7. Utilisation of carbohydrate as an energy source yields an RQ of 1.0. Intermediate values indicate the utilisation of both substrates. The higher the RQ, the greater the carbon dioxide production and hence ventilatory requirement in relation to energy expenditure. A RQ of greater than 1.0 is characteristic of lipogenesis.

Both under- and over-provision of energy is potentially harmful, as also is an inappropriate balance of the two main energy substrates, carbohydrate and fat. The provision of inadequate energy substrates results in utilisation of the body's stores. On the other hand, while the provision of energy (particularly as glucose) in excess of expenditure will replete these stores, it does so at the expense of an increase in RQ. Furthermore, such over-provision, even if accompanied by large amounts of amino acids, may not reverse a net negative nitrogen balance in highly catabolic patients.

Ideally, fat should provide 40-50% of the non-protein energy in ITU patients receiving parenteral nutrition. The use of intravenous fat is only contraindicated by the presence of pre-existing lipaemia, such as is occasionally associated with acute pancreatitis. If fat is being adequately utilised, it is cleared from the circulation and does not interfere with laboratory measurements and measurements made using electrodes with ion-selective membranes. Pharmacological incompatibility of fat emulsions with other components of the nutritional regimen (e.g., 'cracking' of the emulsion in the presence of a high concentration divalent cations) is a theoretical disadvantage, but in practice this is not a problem, provided that the ionic composition of the feed is kept within certain (but generous) limits.

Although the use of fat as an energy source has been linked to the development of various complications (for example, depressed immune function, respiratory dysfunction) such associations are rare and any risk is outweighed by the potential benefits.

NITROGEN

Nitrogen is provided as a balanced mixture of essential and non-essential L-amino acids. Suitable preparations, with a range of concentrations, are available commercially.

There is no clear evidence that the general use of amino acid mixtures enriched with branched chain amino acids confers any clinical benefit. There is, however, convincing evidence that the amino acid glutamine can become essential in the severely ill. Glutamine appears to be particularly important in the nutrition of the small intestinal mucosa but is unstable and is not present in commercially available amino acid preparations. It has been successfully incorporated into stable dipeptides and these have been shown to reverse villous atrophy and decrease gut permeability in patients receiving TPN.

Nitrogen requirements in the severely ill are variable, but usually lie between 0.7 and 1.0 grams per 100 kcals. The use of measurements of plasma protein concentrations as indices of nitrogen balance is vitiated by the rapid fluctuations which can occur due to changes in hydration and to acute phase responses. In theory, measurement of total nitrogen losses should, given knowledge of the intake, allow assessment of nitrogen balance. However, accurate measurement of total urinary nitrogen is technically difficult; measurement of urinary urea is a poor substitute, particularly if the plasma urea concentration is changing or there are additional losses of nitrogen by other routes (e.g., the skin in burns patients). The use of functional tests of nutritional status, for example hand-grip dynamometry, is rarely feasible in patients on an ITU.

Particular care is needed in deciding how much nitrogen to provide to patients in renal failure. Restriction of input is normally required to prevent exacerbation of uraemia but dialysis and other renal replacement techniques increase nitrogen losses and also energy requirements. In the absence of renal failure, severe sepsis or dehydration, an elevated or increasing plasma urea concentration in patients receiving nutritional support suggests the over-provision of amino acids.

WATER

Water is an essential component of a parenteral nutrition regimen, both to satisfy a patient's water requirements and as a vehicle for the various nutrients. It is possible to devise a regimen providing 2000 kcals and 12 g nitrogen in little more than 1500 mL. Patients with renal failure may need to undergo dialysis or haemofiltration to provide 'room' for parenteral nutrition. In general, if a patient has a high fluid requirement (e.g., because of a fistula, diuretic phase of renal failure, etc.) it is simpler not to attempt to provide all the fluid as part of the TPN solution. If this is done, fluid administration can be adjusted in response to any change in requirements without the need to change the rate of infusion of the TPN. Fluid under- or overload is often difficult to diagnose clinically in ITU patients, but the assessment of requirements will be aided by studying pressure data from indwelling catheters (e.g., central venous, pulmonary wedge).

It is important to appreciate that patients on the ITU will often be receiving other intravenous fluids in addition to TPN, and their volume and composition must be taken into account in devising the TPN regimen. Accordingly, meticulous attention is required to the maintenance of fluid balance charts.

MINERALS AND VITAMINS

The plasma concentrations of sodium, potassium, etc., are easily measured. However, sodium concentration is as likely to reflect total extracellular water as sodium; hyponatraemia can only reliably be ascribed to sodium depletion if there are clear clinical signs of a decreased extracellular fluid volume or urinary sodium excretion is low. The assessment of sodium requirements may be aided by its measurement in urine and other fluids being lost.

Potassium and phosphate can be provided empirically, aided by the results of frequent (at least daily during the first few days of TPN), measurements of their plasma concentrations. During the first few days of TPN, there is often a rapid intracellular uptake of potassium and phosphate. Severe, and potentially dangerous, hypophosphataemia is still seen due to a failure to appreciate the importance of adequate phosphate provision from the outset - particularly if an *ad hoc* TPN regimen is prescribed by inexperienced staff. This emphasizes the desirability of nutritional support being prescribed by personnel with appropriate training and experience.

Loss of fluid from the gastrointestinal tract can lead to magnesium deficiency (and consequent resistant hypocalcaemia) and adequate replacement must be given. The trace elements are usually provided using a commercially available 'cocktail' (e.g., Addamel, Additrace - Kabi Pharmacia). The former contains only 10 µmol zinc per vial and one vial daily may provide insufficient zinc to prevent zinc deficiency occurring if TPN needs to be continued for more than 3-4 weeks. Additrace contains 100 µmol zinc per vial and also some elements (e.g., selenium, chromium) not present in Addamel. However, the majority of ITU patients who need TPN require it for relatively short periods and plasma monitoring for trace elements other than zinc is not usually required. It should also be remembered that serum zinc concentrations are poor guides to body zinc content, and that since zinc in the blood is in part bound to albumin, zinc concentration must be considered in the light of the albumin concentration.

Various cocktails of water- and fat-soluble vitamins are also available and should be given as components of TPN from the outset. It is our practice to give an additional 100mg of thiamine when starting TPN; the body stores of this vitamin are limited and may be compromised by pre-existing malnutrition. Alcoholics are particularly at risk. Requirements are increased by the provision of carbohydrate-containing feeds and cases of severe encephalopathy have been reported due to inadequate provision of thiamine. Vitamins are provided on an empirical basis and there is no requirement for biochemical monitoring of vitamin status in patients receiving TPN.

Other components of parenteral feeds

It may be necessary to add insulin to parenteral feeds if patients are diabetic or have acquired insulin resistance due to acidosis or high concentrations of counter-regulatory hormones. However, although insulin is an anabolic hormone, it promotes the conversion of glucose to fat, a process which increases carbon dioxide production and may lead to respiratory embarrassment. If hyperglycaemia occurs, a more appropriate action may be to increase the proportion of energy supplied as fat.

The use of other anabolic agents, e.g., anabolic steroids, growth hormone or IGF-1 (insulin-like growth factor) in parenteral feeding in critically ill patients has received considerable attention recently. Some studies have shown promising results but further work is required.

PREPARATION AND ADMINISTRATION

Parenteral feeds should be administered as nutritionally complete mixtures and prepared in a sterile production unit, either in the local hospital pharmacy or in a commercial facility. There are arguments in favour of both the peripheral and central venous routes for administration. Peripheral cannulae are more easily placed and are free of many of the potential complications of central lines. On the other hand, the latter are preferable for long-term nutritional support (and it may not be possible accurately to predict the likely duration of feeding at the outset). Whichever route is used, it is essential that feeding lines are used for no other purpose, that they are handled as infrequently as possible and then only using a strict aseptic technique.

COMPLICATIONS

The potential complications of TPN are numerous (Table 2.12). They include mechanical problems related to line placement, metabolic complications (discussed below) and sepsis. The first can be minimized by good technique, which requires the application of skills developed through supervised training. The second can be minimized by careful formulation of the feed and appropriate biochemical monitoring. Avoidance of line sepsis requires strict attention to protocols, and in particular to the use of strictly aseptic techniques during line placement and any subsequent manipulation.

Abnormalities of liver function tests are seen frequently in patients on TPN. Most common is an increase in alkaline phosphatase, but the bilirubin may increase to the extent that the patient becomes jaundiced and increases also occur in transaminases. These changes are probably multifactorial in origin. The major contributory factor is usually the provision of energy (either as fat or carbohydrate) in excess of require-

Table 2.12 Potential complications of total parenteral nutrition.

Catheter related

insertion related
- damage to surrounding structures (arteries, nerves)
- pneumothorax

late complications
- displacement
- fracture and embolism
- luminal occlusion
- sepsis
- venous thrombosis

Metabolic
- fluid overload
- hyperglycaemia
- hypoglycaemia (if TPN stopped suddenly)
- hypo/hyperkalaemia
- hypophosphataemia
- specific deficiencies

Hepatobiliary
- abnormal liver function tests
- jaundice

Intestinal
- villous atrophy
- increased permeability

ments, which leads to hepatic steatosis; intrahepatic cholestasis, possibly due to changes in the composition of bile can also occur. However, abnormalities of biochemical liver function tests can be due to many other factors (e.g., sepsis, shock liver) in ITU patients. In adults, TPN-related changes in liver function tests are almost always reversible (e.g., by reduction of energy input or introduction of enteral feeding) but in children, for reasons that are not clear, they can persist and lead to chronic liver disease.

MONITORING

Monitoring of TPN has two purposes - the prevention (or early detection) of complications - and the assessment of response. Clinical monitoring is paramount, but although patients in ITUs are intensively monitored, some important information, e.g., weight, may not be readily obtainable. In the short term, the measurement of anthropometric parameters of nutritional status (e.g., skinfold thicknesses) is of little value and indeed can be compromised by the peripheral oedema that is frequently seen in these patients. As indicated above, plasma protein concentrations (e.g., albumin, retinol-binding protein, prealbumin) are affected by many factors other than nutritional status. Serum IGF-1 (insulin-like growth factor) concentrations offer promise as indicators of the adequacy of nutritional support but are not wholly reliable. Better markers are urgently required, both to assess the response of individuals to nutritional support, and to provide reliable data in trials of different techniques of nutritional support in particular groups of patients to guide future practice.

Both the range of biochemical tests, and the frequency with which they are performed, will be determined by many factors, including the underlying clinical diagnosis and its severity, and range of tests available at the bedside and in the local laboratory. Some general guidance is given in Table 5.2. In general, biochemical monitoring will be required more frequently in the first few days of TPN and in patients who are metabolically unstable; plasma potassium, glucose and phosphate are particularly important. In stable patients, once requirements have been defined, monitoring - at least of metabolic and nutritional status - can be less frequent.

Biochemical monitoring mainly involves the measurement of concentrations of analytes in the serum, and urine. Informed interpretation of the results is essential. This cannot be done in the laboratory, in isolation from the patient; it should be done at the bedside, where the patient can be observed and fluid balance and cumulative charts of results can be studied.

SPECIAL PROBLEMS

Patients on the ITU present special problems with regard to the provision of nutritional support, as alluded to above. In patients with renal failure, energy and nitrogen requirements are increased by dialysis, and it is prudent to provide additional water-soluble vitamins to replace any that may be lost in the dialysate. In patients with respiratory failure, it is important to minimise carbon dioxide production by giving an appropriate amount and balance of energy substrates.

Although the great majority of ITU patients who receive TPN do not develop complications, it should be appreciated that it is a potentially hazardous procedure, and those responsible for its provision should always be alert to the possibility of introducing enteral nutrition. Parenteral support can be continued, at a reduced rate, until full enteral nutrition is established.

FURTHER READING

CARDIOVASCULAR PHYSIOLOGY

Berne RM, Levy MN, Cardiovascular physiology, 1992. St Louis Mosby Year Book.

Tremper KK. Continuous noninvasive cardiac output: Are we getting there? Crit Care Med 1987; **15**: 278-279.

OXYGENATION

Shoemaker WC, Appel P, Bland R. Use of physiological monitoring to predict outcome and to assist in clinical decisions in critically ill postoperative patients. Am J Surg 1983; **146**: 43.

Willis N, Clapham MCC, Mapleson WW. Additional blood gas variables for the rational control of oxygen therapy. Br J Anaes 1987; **59**: 1160.

Hardway RM. Prediction of survival or death of patients in a state of severe shock. Surgery, Gynecology and Obstetrics 1981; **152**: 200-206.

Schumaker PT, Cain SM. The concept of a critical oxygen delivery. Intensive Care Medicine 1987; **13**: 223-229.

Shoemaker WC, Appel PL, Kram HB. Tissue oxygen debt as a determinate of lethal and nonlethal postoperative organ failure. Crit Care Med 1988; **16**: 1117-1120.

Shoemaker WC, Appel PL, Kram HB. Hemodynamic and oxygen transport responses in survivors and non-survivors of high risk surgery. Crit Care Med 1993; **21**: 977-990.

J F Nunn. In: Applied respiratory physiology (3rd edition) Butterworths 1987: 478-494.

METABOLISM AND SHOCK

Clowes GHA, Villee CA. Metabolism in shock (decompensation) In: Hardaway RM (ed) Shock the reversible stage of dying. PSG Publishing Co. Inc. Massachusetts 1988; 31-67.

Kispert P, Caldwell MD. Metabolic changes in sepsis and multiple organ failure. In: Deitch EA (ed). Multiple organ failure. Thieme Medical Publishers, New York. 1988;104-125.

NUTRITIONAL SUPPORT

Andreyev HJN, Forbes A. Parenteral nutrition in adult intensive care. Postgrad Med J 1993; **69**: 841-845.

ASPEN Board of Directors.Guidelines for the use of parenteral and enteral nutrition in adult and paediatric patients. JPEN 1993; **17** (No 4, supplement):1SA-51SA.

Elia M. Artificial nutritional support. Medicine International 1990; **82**:3392-3396.

Payne-James J, Wicks C. Key Facts in Clinical Nutrition. Edinburgh, Churchill Livingstone 1994.

Pichard C, Jeejeebhoy KN. Nutritional management of clinical undernutrition. In: Garrow JS, James WPT (eds) Human Nutrition and Dietetics (9th edition). Edinburgh, Churchill Livingstone 1991: 21-439.

Marshall WJ, Peri-operative nutritional support. Care Crit Ill 1994; **10**: 163-167.

Chapter 3

Organs in shock

THE LUNGS

Acute lung injury starts early in shock. The degree of injury will depend on the cause and extent of the shock. In septic shock, leucocytes are deposited in the lung with the release of potent mediators causing lung injury. This injury is manifested as an increase in permeability of the lung microvasculature. This allows pulmonary oedema to develop even with low venous pressures.

When severe, the acute lung injury progresses to the clinical picture of adult respiratory distress syndrome (ARDS). There are many synonyms for ARDS including 'Shock Lung' and 'Vietnam Lung'. ARDS is associated with a mortality exceeding 50%. ARDS can be defined as respiratory insufficiency due to interstitial pulmonary oedema resulting from increased pulmonary capillary permeability. It is probably the pulmonary manifestation of a generalised abnormality of cellular function. ARDS is a clinical syndrome with the following features:

- severe hypoxaemia (PaO_2 <8.0 kPa on 40% inspired oxygen and at least 5 cm H_2O positive end-expiratory pressure (PEEP))
- radiological appearance of bilateral pulmonary infiltrates
- reduced lung compliance (<30 mL/cm H_2O)
- a pulmonary artery wedge pressure (< 18 mmHg), if plasma oncotic pressure is normal. (This criterion excludes cardiogenic and hydrostatic causes of pulmonary oedema)

ARDS is rarely an isolated problem and is usually associated with multiple organ failure.

Table 3.1 Causes of adult respiratory distress syndrome

Category	Causes
• Trauma	- Burns - Post traumatic embolism - Lung contusion - Near drowing
• Sepsis	- Bacterial / viral, fungal pneumonia - Gram negative sepsis
• Toxic	- Smoke inhalation - Aspiration of gastric juice - Inhalation of corrosive chemicals - Chronic inspiration of high oxygen tensions
• Hypovolaemic shock	- Haemorrhage - Septic shock - Cardiogenic shock - Anaphylactic shock
• Miscellaneous	- Pancreatitis - Multiple transfusions - Drug ingestion - Eclampsia - Bowel infarction

PATHOPHYSIOLOGY

Although the precise chain of events leading from the initial pulmonary injury to the development of ARDS is unknown, the end result is an inflammatory reaction which results in increased permeability of the alveolar-capillary membrane. This allows the development of pulmonary oedema despite no increase in pulmonary venous pressure. Ventilation-perfusion imbalance increases shunting and leads to hypoxaemia. The lungs become stiff (decreased compliance), increasing the work required for breathing. Functional residual capacity falls and alveolar collapse and closure of airways further contribute to the hypoxaemia. Table 3.1 classifies some of the commoner causes of ARDS.

CLINICAL FEATURES

Dyspnoea is usually the first symptom. Tachypnoea leads to hypocapnia which may lead to peripheral vasoconstriction although in septic shock, vasodilatation is usual, and the peripheries are warm. Clinical signs of pulmonary oedema are present. There is also frequently evidence of multiple organ failure.

There is characteristically a latent period of a few hours between the causative insult and the development of clinical features of ARDS, whereafter progression is rapid and urgent intervention is required.

INVESTIGATIONS

Arterial blood gas analysis will reveal the hypoxaemia and, usually, hypocapnia. The latter produces a left shift in the oxyhaemoglobin dissociation curve, potentially increasing oxygen delivery to the tissues so that cyanosis may not be present despite the hypoxaemia. The radiological appearances are characteristic, although non-specific. Serial radiology is vital to detect possible complications (e.g., pneumothorax) although the radiological appearances are not necessarily a good guide to the severity of the functional disorder.

Haemodynamic monitoring (pulmonary artery occlusion pressure or wedge pressure measurements) are required to confirm the diagnosis and to monitor fluid replacement.

MANAGEMENT

The principles of management are aimed at supporting the patient while the underlying condition is treated. In relation to respiratory function, this essentially entails enrichment of the inspired gas with oxygen to maintain PaO_2, and oxygen saturation of haemoglobin, and maintenance of a sufficient positive airways pressure to overcome the decreased compliance and prevent alveolar collapse, without producing oxygen toxicity or barotrauma.

Techniques for achieving this (see Table 3.2) range from the use of a high flow, tightly fitting face mask, which may be adequate in mild cases through various techniques of artificial ventilation. Exceptionally, extracorporeal membrane oxygenation (ECMO) and carbon dioxide removal may be a last resort.

Maintenance of adequate fluid balance is essential. 'Adequate' in this context requires a balance between the desirability of reducing circulating fluid volume to limit the generation of pulmonary oedema, and the need to adjust cardiac filling pressures sufficient for adequate cardiac output. This latter is an essential requirement for the maintenance of adequate tissue oxygen delivery.

Table 3.2 Major techniques of mechanical or assisted ventilation

Technique		Comments
• ***Intermittent negative pressure ventilation***	INPV	
- cuirass		
- iron lung		Still used by some patients with respiratory failure due to poliomyelitis but not used in ITUs
• ***Intermittent positive pressure ventilation***	IPPV	
- continuous positive airways pressure	CPAP	With a tightly fitting face mask or with endotracheal intubation
- nasal IPPV		Patient-triggered through a nasal mask
- controlled mandatory ventilation	CMV	All the respiratory work is done by the ventilator; spontaneous breathing not possible
- intermittent mandatory ventilation	IMV	Spontaneous breathing is possible, but the ventilator takes over if a breath is not initiated by the patient within a preset time
- pressure support ventilation	PSV	The patient's spontaneous breathing is augmented by a fixed amount of positive pressure
- high frequency jet ventilation	HFJV	Small volumes of gas are moved in and out of the lungs at very high frequency

Cardiovascular function will often be impaired by the underlying cause of ARDS, and further impaired by positive pressure ventilation techniques, which increase intra-thoracic pressure and impair the venous return. Inotropic support may be required. Associated disorders, e.g., renal failure, will require appropriate management, and care must be taken to treat and avoid infection and maintain nutritional status (if fluid balance allows).

RESPIRATORY SUPPORT

Respiratory support is required for patients with respiratory failure (defined as $PaO_2 < 8$ kPa with or without $PaCO_2 > 6.7$ kPa when breathing room air at sea level). ARDS is one of many causes of respiratory failure, the more important of which are listed in Table 3.3. Respiratory support is frequently provided prophylactically following major (especially cardiothoracic) surgery.

The general principles of respiratory support are to maintain the PaO_2 by ensuring an adequate inspired oxygen tension and reducing ventilation-perfusion imbalance, and to control $PaCO_2$ by providing adequate alveolar ventilation.

The decision to start mechanical ventilation is not always a straightforward one. It is mandatory in a patient who is apnoeic but for post operative patients it is likely to depend on local policies related to the extent of the surgical procedure. Even less well defined is which mode of ventilation should be used. The earliest technique to be widely employed in ITUs was continuous mandatory ventilation (CMV), in which the ventilator does all the breathing. Many newer techniques have been devised but ventilator technology has moved faster than its rational application. There are now many different techniques for mechanical

Table 3.3 Causes of respiratory failure requiring mechanical ventilation

• Central depression	- sedative/analgesic drugs - cerebral ischaemia
• Neurological	- cervical cord lesions - phrenic nerve lesions
• Musculoskeletal	- muscle wasting - damage to the thoracic cage (flail chest)
• Lung parenchyma	- pneumonia - ARDS - emphysema - chronic obstructive airways disease
• Preventative	- postoperative - haemodynamic instability

ventilation but appropriate matching of technique to particular respiratory disorder has not yet been achieved.

THE KIDNEYS

The kidneys are regulatory organs that are essential for preservation of the volume and composition of body fluids. Renal control of the excretion of water and solutes such as hydrogen ions, sodium, potassium, and calcium is essential for preservation of the extracellular, and ultimately the intracellular, environment. These tasks are mediated by a complex interaction of neural, hormonal, metabolic and haemodynamic factors which act in concert to maintain homeostasis. When the capacity of renal compensatory mechanisms is exceeded, homeostasis begins to fail and the patient begins to develop renal failure.

Following shock, defined at the cellular level as 'an interruption in the delivery of nutrients and removal of metabolites', the homeostatic mechanisms are directed to preserve the function of organs essential for immediate survival (brain, heart and lungs). This process is at the expense of those organs such as the gastrointestinal tract, kidney and skin, for which decreased perfusion presents a less immediate threat to life, although preservation of the latter's function in the longer term is just as critical.

Decreased renal perfusion occurs within minutes of the shock-inducing event, is proportional to the severity of the insult and, if it remains untreated, is the first step in the path towards acute renal failure.

RENAL RESPONSE TO REDUCED PERFUSION

Renal haemodynamics

The kidneys normally receive 25% of the cardiac output (1300 mL/min) which falls to less than 4% (200 mL/min) in severe hypovolaemia; this represents an important reserve blood supply in shock. Glomerular filtration depends upon an adequate renal perfusion pressure of at least 50-60 mmHg to overcome the oncotic and hydrostatic pressure opposing filtration at the glomerular membrane. Under normal conditions, glomerular filtration is preserved across a range of blood pressures by an autoregulatory system affecting the muscle tone of the afferent and efferent arterioles in reponse to several neural and hormonal mediators

Table. 3.4 Factors influencing renovascular resistance

- Increased renovascular resistance (vasoconstriction)
  - Angiotensin II
  - Alpha adrenergic hormones
  - Renal autonomic nerve supply
  - Thromboxane A2
  - Vasopressin
- Decreased renovascular resistance (vasodilatation)
  - Prostaglandins (PGE2, PGI2)
  - Atrial natriuretic peptides

(Table 3.4). The renovascular resistance to blood flow is the net result of these processes.

In mild hypovolaemia, glomerular filtration is maintained by a decrease in the afferent arteriolar resistance, thus maintaining the intraglomerular pressure despite a fall in perfusion pressure. However if more severe hypovolaemia ensues, and perfusion pressure falls below 50-60 mm Hg, renovascular resistance rises due to vasoconstriction, and glomerular filtration falls precipitatously.

Renal hypoperfusion stimulates the release of renin from the juxtoglomerular cells, yielding angiotensin II, a potent vasoconstrictor, which helps to maintain blood pressure in hypovolaemia, and within the kidney causes efferent arteriolar constriction, thus maintaining intraglomerular pressure despite reduced perfusion pressure (see Chapter 2).

Hypovolaemia following shock produces a systemic vasoconstriction which is mediated by the renin-angiotensin system, catecholamines, the autonomic nervous system and thromboxane. Within the kidney, these vasoconstrictor pathways are balanced by intrarenal prostaglandin release which has a protective vasodilatory function and maintains some level of renal blood flow during systemic vasoconstriction. (For this reason the use of non-steroidal anti-inflammatory drugs which inhibit cyclo-oxygenase and hence vasodilatory prostaglandins, can produce severe reduction in glomerular filtration in hypovolaemic patients).

As renal perfusion pressure falls below the minimum required for filtration, glomerular filtration ceases. Thus, as perfusion pressure falls in shock, the initial preservation of glomerular filtration by efferent vasoconstriction becomes destructive as cortical perfusion is progressively shut off. This process represents a continuum along a common pathway extending from reduced renal perfusion to pre-renal uraemia and finally acute renal failure.

Renal Sodium and Water Handling

Homeostatic mechanisms within the kidney are directed towards salt and water retention in order to maintain or restore the circulating blood volume. The following mechanisms have been identified:

- *Increased sodium reabsorption:*

  Angiotensin II mediated aldosterone release promotes sodium reabsorption in the distal convoluted tubules and collecting ducts. Renal nerve stimulation also increases tubular sodium reabsorption.

  Intrarenal shunting of blood from outer cortical nephrons to inner juxtaglomerular nephrons, which plunge into the hyperosmolar renal medulla, enhance sodium reabsorption.

- *Increased water reabsorption:*

  Angiotensin II mediated efferent arteriolar vasoconstriction increases the filtered fraction at the glomerulus and thus increases the protein content of the blood in the efferent arteriole. This increases the oncotic pressure in the peritubular capillaries, increasing proximal tubular reabsorption of water.

  Antidiuretic hormone (ADH) is released in response to increased plasma osmolality, decreased extracellular fluid volume and reduced blood pressure. ADH, along with angiotensin II, promotes water reabsorption across the osmotic gradient within the collecting duct and may also promote sodium reabsorption in the ascending loop of Henle and the collecting ducts. Antidiuretic hormone also acts as a vasoconstrictor.

The net result of these mechanisms in shock is the retention of water, sodium and chloride, and the production of urine with low sodium content (less than 20 mmol/L), low volume and high osmolality. Although there will be some retention of nitrogenous products (urea and creatinine), this is a protective phenomenon as a direct result of impaired renal perfusion and does not reflect a problem with the kidneys. This state is sometimes termed 'pre-renal failure'. In experimental models of haemorrhagic hypovolaemia, reduced urinary sodium excretion can be detected within 30 minutes. However, these findings are confounded if diuretics or hypertonic fluids (e.g., mannitol) have been administered. If renal underperfusion is severe immediate anuria may ensue. Restoration of normal renal function is most likely if the period of hypovolaemia is short, and resuscitation is carried out promptly. The greater the delay in resuscitation, the greater the risk of intrinsic acute renal failure developing.

Acid Base Homeostasis

Under normal circumstances the kidney excretes about 75 mmol of hydrogen ions per 24 h via three mechanisms.

- Direct excretion of hydrogen ions – 0.1 mmol/24 h.
- Excretion of buffers such as K_2HPO_4 – 35 mmol/24 h.
- Excretion of ammonium ions derived from glutamine – 40 mmol/24 h.[1]

Sodium and bicarbonate are filtered at the glomerulus and sodium is reabsorbed by the renal tubule in exchange for hydrogen ions. Bicarbonate cannot pass directly across the wall of the renal tubule but secreted hydrogen ions combine with bicarbonate to form carbonic acid, which then dissociates into carbon dioxide and water. Carbon dioxide diffuses into the tubule cell and is reincorporated into bicarbonate by the action of carbonate dehydratase (Fig 3.1).

In hypovolaemic acidosis, there is decreased delivery of sodium ions to the distal convoluted tubule which limits the amount of hydrogen ions

[1] It has been argued that ammonium excretion does not constitute a route for net disposal of nitrogen. Since urea synthesis entails hydrogen ion formation from ammonium, the apparent excretion of hydrogen ions buffered in ammonium is balanced by decreased hydrogen ion formation in the body.

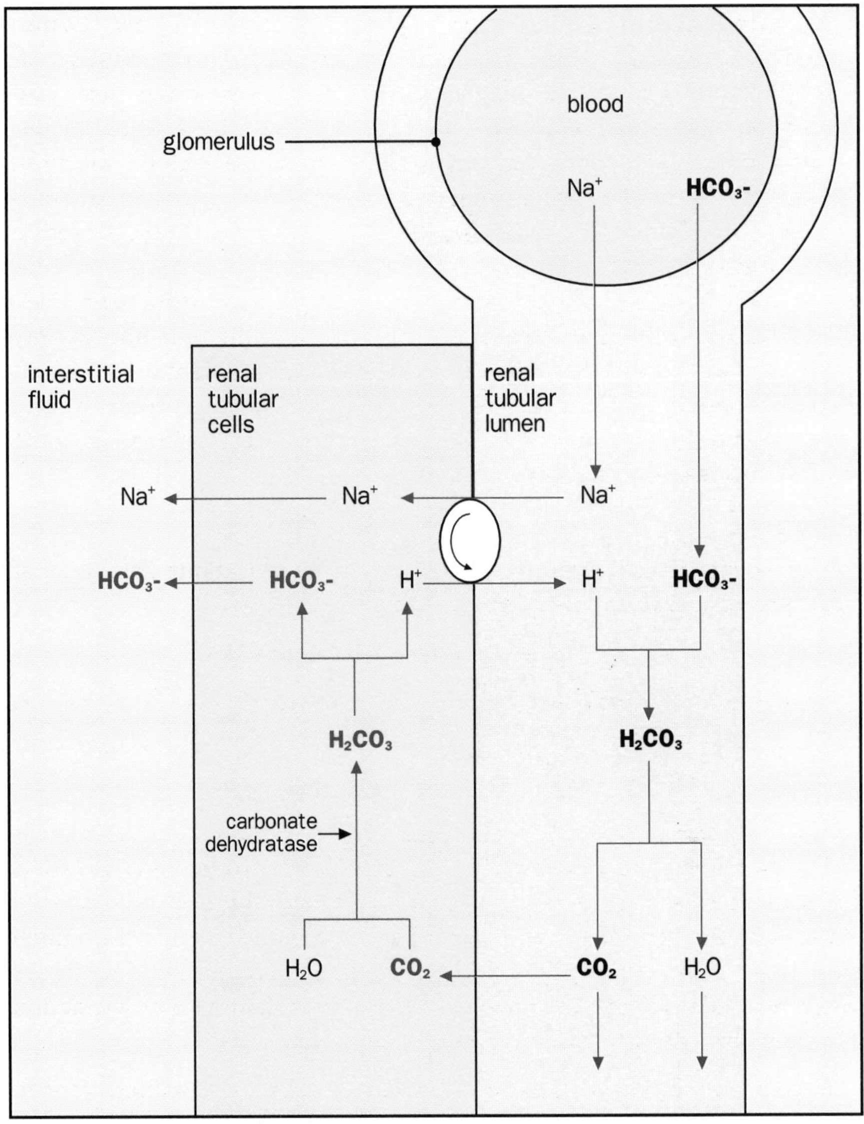

Figure 3.1 Reabsorption of filtered bicarbonate by renal tubular cells.

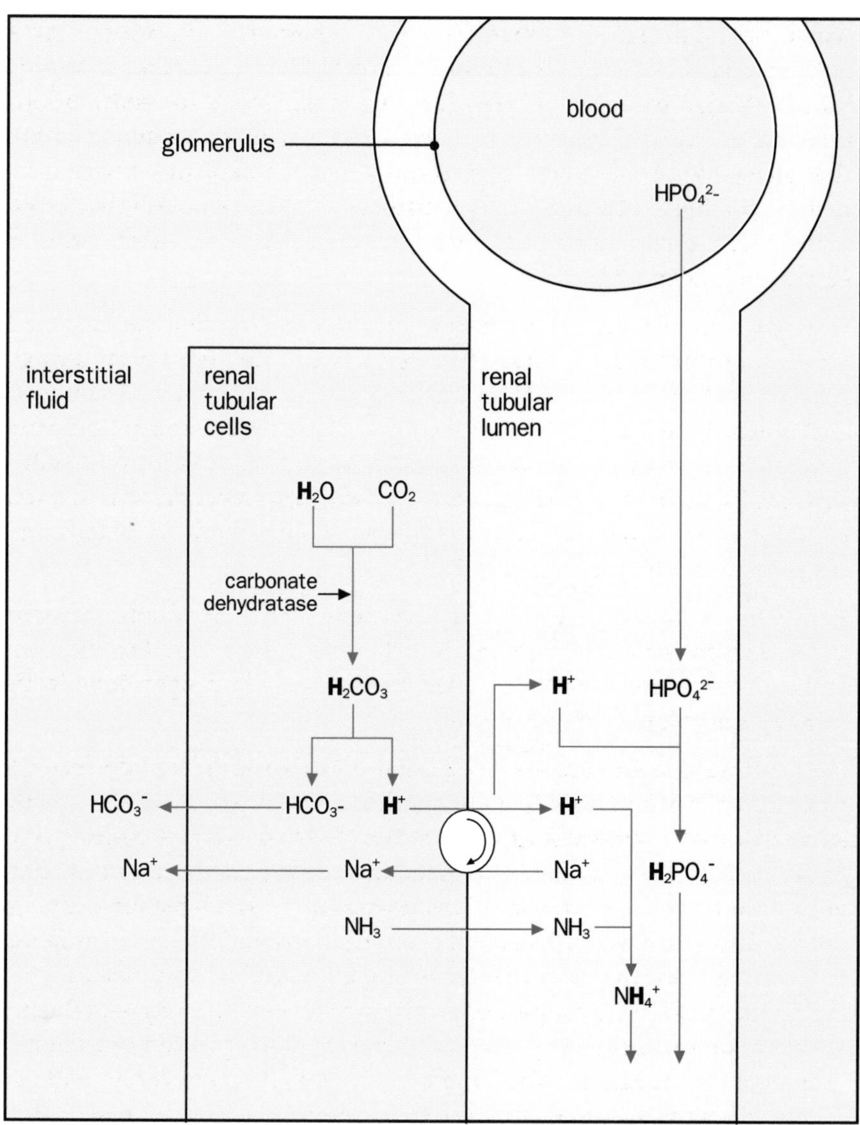

Figure 3.2 Renal hydrogen ion excretion.

which can be excreted. Systemic acidosis, whether respiratory or metabolic in origin, increases the amount of hydrogen ions secreted into the tubular lumen by proximal tubular cells in exchange for sodium ions, thus increasing sodium reabsorption. The increased hydrogen ion secretion increases the amount of carbonic acid formed and hence more carbon dioxide is produced which diffuses into the renal tubular cells to form bicarbonate again. In this way bicarbonate reabsorption is increased in acidosis.

However, increased reabsorption of filtered bicarbonate does not replenish bicarbonate stores which have been depleted by buffering a non-respiratory acidosis. New bicarbonate is formed when ammonia and phosphate buffer hydrogen ions. Ammonia production from glutamine increases in acidosis, and secreted ammonia buffers hydrogen ions in the form of ammonium ions. Tubular phosphate reabsorption is inhibited in acidosis and this may also provide additional buffering capacity for hydrogen ions (Fig 3.2).

Thus the renal response to hypovolaemia and metabolic acidosis involve retention of sodium and bicarbonate in exchange for hydrogen and potassium ions, and increased excretion of hydrogen ions in the form of ammonium and phosphate salts.

In respiratory acidosis, the accumulation of carbon dioxide leads to increased intrarenal bicarbonate synthesis which compensates for the acidosis due to retention of carbon dioxide. If there is a deficiency of potassium in addition to hypovolaemia (due for example to treatment with diuretics or to diarrhoea), less potassium is available for exchange with sodium ions within the renal tubule and instead increased amounts of hydrogen ions are excreted in exchange for sodium ions, leading to a metabolic alkalosis and paradoxically acidic urine. In hyperkalaemic states, potassium excretion supervenes over hydrogen ion excretion in exchange for sodium ions and there is a tendency to metabolic acidosis. These changes depend upon the kidney's ability to respond to homeostatic signals and in acute renal failure these compensatory mechanisms fail, resulting in hyperkalaemia and acidosis.

Renal Nitrogen Excretion

The normal adult excretes about 8-16g of nitrogen each day, of which urea represents approximately 85% (250-500 mmol/24h) and creatinine

5% (9-17 mmol/24h). A proportion of urea filtered at the glomerulus is reabsorbed, a process that supports the osmotic gradient between the renal cortex and medulla required for the maintenance of the kidney's concentrating mechanism. During renal hypoperfusion, tubular reabsorption of filtered urea increases, and plasma urea concentrations tend to rise. In contrast, creatinine is both filtered by the glomerulus and secreted into the renal tubule from the peritubular capillaries. For this reason creatinine excretion, and therefore plasma creatinine concentrations, are less affected by renal hypoperfusion than urea. The disproportionate increase in plasma urea concentrations in shock is also a reflection of increased ureagenesis arising from shock-induced proteolysis. Occasionally large increases in serum creatinine concentration may be seen in patients with massive muscle destruction such as in crush injury, rhabdomyolysis or electrical burns. Nevertheless, a disproportionate rise in plasma urea concentration compared with that of creatinine is a useful pointer to the diagnosis of a hypovolaemic pre-renal state.

Increased urinary urea excretion is detectable within 12-24 hours of shock and provided renal function remains stable, can be used as a crude indicator of nitrogen excretion. Plasma and urine creatinine concentrations are much less susceptible to the effect of proteolysis. However, serial measurements of urinary creatinine excretion in critically ill patients do show a consistent fall, reflecting the reduction in muscle mass from which urinary creatinine is principally derived. This is a very gradual process, and does not prevent the use of serial creatinine measurements as an indication of glomerular filtration on a day-to-day basis.

PATTERNS OF RESPONSE IN SHOCK - INDUCED ACUTE RENAL IMPAIRMENT

Pre-Renal Insufficiency

This is the most common cause of increased plasma urea concentration and arises from diminished renal perfusion. The renal response to underperfusion from any cause is similar. The of causes of renal hypoperfusion are given in Table 3.5.

Table 3.5 Causes of renal hypoperfusion

• Decreased volume due to	- dehydration - blood loss - extra-cellular extra vascular fluid accumulation (ascites, etc)
• Circulatory failure	- septic shock - heart failure with decreased cardiac output
• Renovascular	- renal artery occlusion - renal vein thrombosis

Biochemical features

Plasma sodium concentrations are either normal or increased in dehydration, but tend to be low in heart failure, septic shock, ascites and other conditions associated with extravascular fluid accumulation. In all cases of renal hypoperfusion, plasma urea concentrations tend to be increased with normal or only moderate increases in plasma creatinine concentration. Urinary sodium is generally less than 20 mmol/L, with a sodium/potassium ratio of less than one. Sodium retention also occurs during the first three days following serious burn injury irrespective of fluid and sodium administration. Occassionally low urinary sodium excretion may be simply due to a low sodium intake. Sodium conservation in pre-renal states may not be observed in patients receiving diuretics or hyperosmolar solutions such as mannitol. Urine osmolality is higher than that of plasma, and urine flow rates are typically less than 1 mL/kg/min. Urine analysis reveals only hyaline or granular casts and clinical albuminuria (greater than 200 mg/L) is usually absent.

Post-Renal Causes of Renal Insufficiency

Any acute obstruction of the urinary outflow can be described as post-renal insufficiency. This includes ureteric obstructions caused by stones, strictures or blood clots, and urethral blockages due to trauma, prostatic hypertrophy, etc. Biochemical investigations are not of great help in such patients other than in the evaluation of the extent of renal impairment. Patients with suspected post-renal insufficiency should have examination by ultrasound and, where indicated, be catheterised. Catheterisation generally yields a large volume of urine and allows accurate assessment of subsequent urine flow. However, bladder rupture can be associated with urinary leak into the peritoneal cavity resulting in autodialysis into the blood stream of the urinary contents. Plasma concentrations of urea, creatinine and potassium will be high, and rapidly return to normal following drainage and bladder repair.

Intrinsic Renal Impairment

The mechanisms leading to shock-induced intrinsic renal failure are complex. Although a broad classification has been attempted below, elements of all mechanisms are likely to be involved to some extent in the development of renal impairment.

Renal Ischaemia

Intrinsic renal damage is likely to occur when pre-renal impairment with severe vasoconstriction is allowed to persist. The renal medulla is particularly susceptible since medullary blood flow may not return to normal for some time after treatment of hypovolaemia and the medulla has a high metabolic rate requiring high rates of substrate delivery.

Glomerular Failure

Prolonged ischaemia will result in glomerular damage, leading to a reduction in glomerular filtration rate despite adequate resuscitation. Prolonged renal hypoperfusion, with persistent renin and angiotensin release and vasoconstriction, lead to ischaemia-induced microvascular damage, which current free radical theory suggests will be exacerbated following reperfusion. Glomerular membrane damage will result in plasma protein leakage into the filtrate which may further compromise tubular function.

Bacterial endotoxin is associated with initial vasodilatation followed by vasoconstriction mediated by the sympathetic nervous system, renin - angiotensin system and catecholamines. These processes increase cell membrane permeability and can potentiate disseminated intravascular coagulation. Thus a septic episode will enhance vasoconstriction and a shift of fluid from the extra-cellular space into the cells making shock-induced hypovolaemia worse. Theoretically, the kidney may be at a greater risk from sepsis than other organs because of its concentrating ability which may result in higher concentrations within the kidney of both bacterial toxins and toxic antibiotics such as aminoglycosides

Table 3.6 Summary of nephrotoxic drugs *

Drug class	Examples
• Antifungal agents	- amphotericin
• Aminoglycoside antibiotics	- amikacin - gentamicin - kanamycin - neomycin - netilmicin - tobramycin
• Other antibiotics	- vancomycin - colistin
• Chemotherapeutics	- cisplatin - methotrexate
• Drugs used in rheumatoid arthritis	- gold - penicillamine

* The above examples are known as nephrotoxic drugs; other drugs such as non-steroidal anti-inflammatory agents and analgesics may be deleterious to renal function under certain circumstances. The reader is refered to the appropriate texts including the current edition of the British National Formulary.

(Table 3.6). In severe sepsis there may be no alternative to the use of nephrotoxic antibiotics, but plasma concentrations should be monitored and doses modified to avoid excessively high plasma concentrations.

Tubular obstruction and failure

Interruption of the delivery of substrates to, and removal of metabolites from the kidney, due to ischaemia and nephrotoxins (both microbial and arising from antibacterial treatment), can block normal tubular metabolism and lead to tubular cell damage. This includes tubular cell swelling, loss of microvilli and cell desquamation, all of which can obstruct the tubular lumen, thus preventing the passage of glomerular filtrate, resulting in the formation of characteristic tubular casts. Even in the absence of tubular blockage, tubular epithelial cell damage leads to reduced reabsorptive capacity. This situation can be exacerbated if large amounts of protein such as haemoglobin, myoglobin or myeloma proteins reach the tubule. At a time when the flow of filtrate is low, there is a greater risk of precipitation of these proteins. For this reason, maintenance of a high urine flow rate by vigorous administration of fluids is required to reduce the risk of tubular blockage.

BIOCHEMICAL FEATURES OF INTRINSIC RENAL FAILURE

Oliguric and Anuric Renal Impairment

Plasma sodium concentrations are normal or low due to fluid retention from reduced renal excretion and from the osmotic effects of uraemia drawing fluid from the intracellular compartment. Inappropriate fluid administration and the generation of endogenous water from metabolism may also contribute to dilutional hyponatraemia. Plasma potassium concentrations are normal or high because of the loss of intracellular potassium due to catabolism, acidaemia and due to reduced renal excretion. Urea and creatinine concentrations in plasma tend to rise in parallel. Plasma magnesium, urate and phosphate concentrations are also likely to be increased, due to reduced renal excretion.

Where urine is produced, the sodium concentration tends to be greater than 20 mmol/L (sodium/potassium ratio greater than 1.0) and urine osmolality is often close to that of plasma, indicating the absence of renal concentrating ability. Clinical albuminuria is usually present (greater than 200 mg/L of albumin). Urinary sediment frequently contains tubular epithelial cells both free and in the form of casts together with characteristic course granular casts. Haematuria may also be present, together with red cell casts, particularly in patients with glomerulonephritis.

Polyuric renal impairment

In general this condition is less common than oliguric renal failure but can be confusing, since urine output is normal or increased with low sodium content. Despite the preservation of urinary flow, plasma urea and creatinine concentrations are frequently at the levels seen in oliguric renal failure. This state may accompany severe liver disease or follow oliguric renal failure and represent the diuretic phase of recovery, or may occur in patients in whom oliguria or anuria were never a feature. Urinary sodium concentration is often low, indicating the survival of tubular sodium reabsorptive ability, but the osmolality of the urine is low, unlike pre-renal states. The high plasma osmolality (due to uraemia) and low urinary osmolality can lead to confusion of this type of renal impairment with diabetes insipidus. It should be possible to exclude diabetes insipidus by careful consideration of the history and fluid balance over the preceding days together with haemodynamic monitoring (e.g., central venous pressure monitoring to exclude inappropriate diuresis with hypovolaemia). Where fluid balance studies indicate a net fluid accumulation, such patients should have sufficient fluid replacement to avoid hypovolaemia and any further renal injury, but a negative fluid balance should be maintained until either the patient starts to produce a more concentrated urine, or is deemed to be euvolaemic by haemodynamic indicators.

Polyuric renal failure has a better prognosis than oliguric failure provided fluid balance is maintained without complications.

PRINCIPLES OF MANAGEMENT OF SHOCK-INDUCED RENAL FAILURE AND THE ROLE OF LABORATORY MONITORING

The purpose of the following summary of the management principles of acute renal failure is to allow laboratory monitoring to be seen in context. For detailed descriptions of the practical aspects of the management of renal failure, the reader is referred to more specialised texts.

Following a shock inducing event (e.g., sepsis, surgery, trauma, burns, pancreatitis, etc.) renal failure may occur immediately or develop insidiously over the subsequent hours and days, in either case the investigational steps are summarised in Fig 3.3.

Sodium and fluid balance

In a patient with renal impairment the careful and accurate assessment of sodium, potassium and fluid balance over the preceding hours or days is an important component in the patient's evaluation. Allowance should be made for endogenous water production of between 500 and 1000 mL/24h in the adult, and insensible losses of between 0.5 and 0.6 mL/kg/h. The latter rises in febrile patients by approximately 300 mL/day/°C. Negative fluid balance will be found in patients with renal impairment due to dehydration, whilst patients with hypovolaemia due to extravascular fluid accumulation (such as in ascites, heart failure or septic shock) will tend to be in positive fluid balance. Patients with oliguric intrinsic renal failure will also tend to be in positive fluid balance.

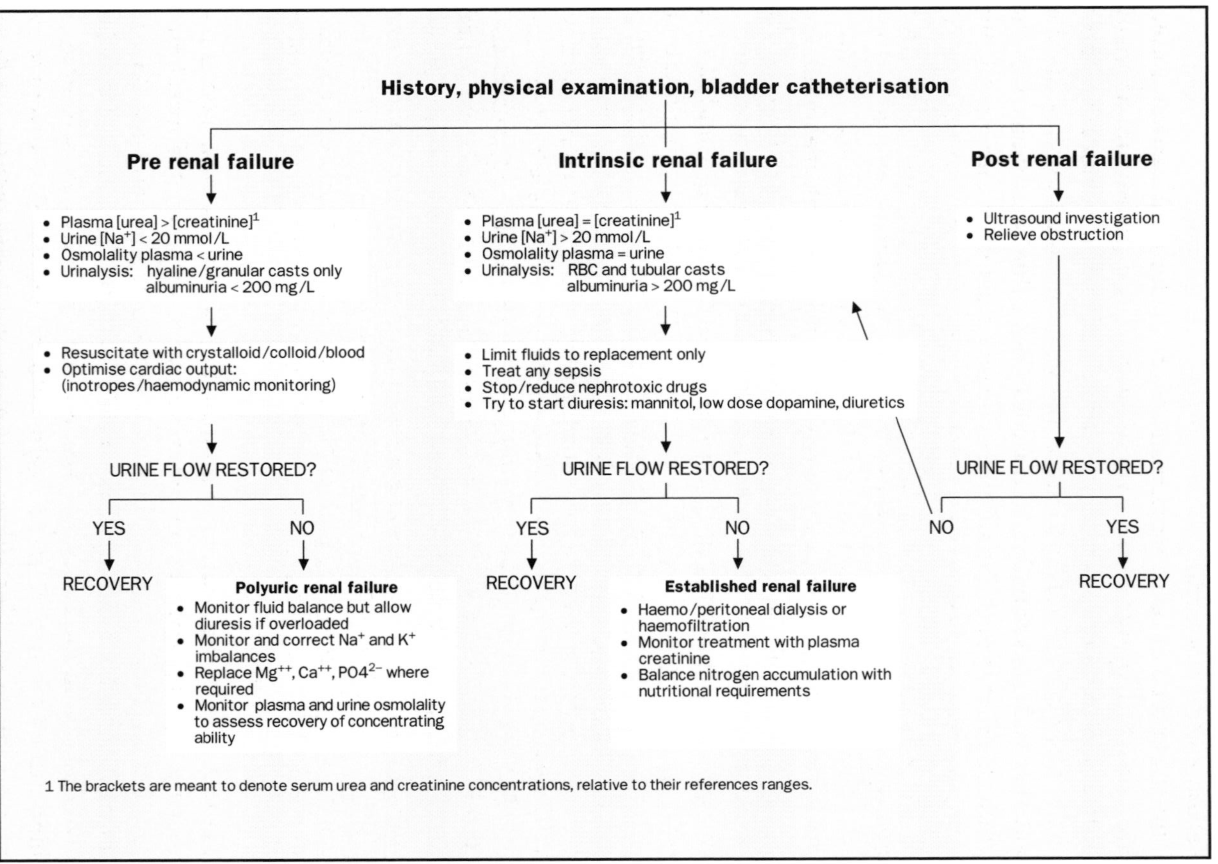

Figure 3.3 Principles of management of shock-induced renal failure

Haemodynamic monitoring

Whilst the type of renal impairment in the majority of patients can be identified by clinical assessment and by laboratory investigations, many critically ill patients require invasive haemodynamic monitoring. These include patients with heart failure, burns, severe trauma or sepsis and patients with severe oedema or ascites where fluid accumulates in the extra-vascular space. The simplest haemodynamic measurement is the assessment of central venous pressure by introducing a cannula via the subclavian vein. Normal or high central venous pressures would rule out hypovolaemic states, whilst low fluid pressures would suggest significant hypovolaemia. More information can be obtained by introduction of a Swann-Ganz catheter via the subclavian, internal jugular or femoral vein. This is a multilumen catheter which passes through the right atrium and right ventricle into a pulmonary artery, allowing measurement of pulmonary wedge pressure, left atrial pressure and cardiac output (see Chapter 2). Cardiac output is measured by thermodilution, which involves injection of a bolus of cold saline into the right atrium via one of the lumens of the catheter and measurement of the transit time for the saline to reach a thermistor located in the pulmonary artery. With these data, fluid requirements can be accurately assessed in order to optimise cardiac output. In pre-renal impairment, reduced cardiac output due to low filling pressures would be anticipated, and correction of hypovolaemia with appropriate volumes of fluid should increase filling pressures and improve cardiac output. In intrinsic renal failure, normal or high filling pressures are likely to be found due to fluid retention. The benefit the patient obtains from haemodynamic monitoring must be balanced against the risk of sepsis associated with these invasive techniques.

Maintenance or restoration of a normal or high urine flow rate is the major goal in the prevention and treatment of acute renal failure. Urine production indicates some degree of renal perfusion and the flow of glomerular filtrate through the tubules reduces the risks of tubular swelling due to the effects of nephrotoxins and previous ischaemia. A high urine flow rate, protects against blocking of tubules with precipitated proteins and debris by increasing solubility and reduces the duration of exposure of the tubules to nephrotoxins during urine concentration.

In the critically ill, there is often a conflict of priorities between vigorous fluid administration to maintain a good urine flow, and the function of other organs such as the heart and lungs which may be put at risk by fluid loading. The skilled ITU physician will balance the risk of 'keeping a patient dry', to avoid pulmonary or cardiac complications, with the risk of acute renal failure due, for example, to a septic episode in a patient whose renal function is bordering on pre-renal impairment. This is a common situation in which laboratory data are an essential component of the decision making process. Prevention of intrinsic renal failure is preferable to treatment, and early recognition of renal impairment is aided by accurate and serial measurements of plasma and urine biochemistry. A falling urinary sodium excretion with a rising plasma urea concentration is frequently an early feature of impending hypovolaemia due, for example, to sepsis, under-resuscitation or occult bleeding.

Hyperphosphataemia is common in the critically ill with acute renal failure due both to reduced renal excretion and release of phosphate from necrotic tissue. Although patients tolerate mild to moderate hyperphosphataemia reasonably well, hypocalcaemia due to calcium sequestration by phosphate may be a problem. Treatment involves removal of necrotic tissue and low phosphate nutritional regimes. Phosphate will be removed by dialysis or haemofiltration. Hypophosphataemia is sometimes found in critically ill patients with polyuric renal failure due to increased urinary losses as well as to the effects of insulin shifting phosphate into the intracellular space, particularly if calories are being provided by hypertonic dextrose solutions. Treatment with intravenous potassium acid phosphate may be indicated.

Whilst hypermagnesaemia frequently occurs in acute renal failure due to reduced excretion, hypomagnesaemia can also occur due to excessive urinary losses because of nephrotoxic tubular damage which reduces tubular reabsorption. Severe hypomagnesaemia compromises the action of parathroid hormone and requires correction.

Hyperkalaemia is a major biochemical problem in acute renal failure and may become clinically manifest when plasma concentrations are greater than 6.0 mmol/L with characteristic ECG changes. If severe hyperkalaemia goes uncorrected then ventricular fibrillation and cardiac arrest are likely. In critically ill patients with renal failure,

Table 3.7 Summary of the types of renal replacement therapies

• **Continuous Arteriovenous Haemofiltration (CAVH)**	
Principle:	Passage of arterial blood through a hollow fibre filter under positive pressure. Plasma ultrafiltrate is lost which is replaced intravenously with fluid containing appropriate solutes.
Clearance rate:	10 mL/min
Advantages:-	Easy to set up in Intensive Care, modest blood flow of 200 mL/min needed, only moderate training required, allows fluid overload to be corrected
Disadvantages:-	Specialised equipment needed, arterial and venous access needed, filtration stops with hypotension. Not as efficient as CAVHD, complex i.v. replacement, poor control of hyperkalaemia. TPN possible.
• **Continous Arteriovenous Haemodiafiltration (CAVHD)**	
Principle:	As for CAVH but filter is also in contact with contra-flowing dialysate solution.
Clearance rate:	30 mL/min
Advantages:	Higher clearances, simpler replacement fluids, good control of hyperkalaemia. Works provided systolic blood pressure > 60 mmHg. Can correct most metabolic abnormalities due to renal failure. TPN possible
Disadvantages:	Few compared with CAVH
• **Intermittent Haemodialysis (IHD)**	
Principle:	Passage of blood and dialysate on either side of a semipermeable membrane.
Clearance rate:	>30 mL/min
Advantages:	More efficient solute removal, used for long term treatment.
Disadvantages:	Because used intermittently can cause dangerous osmolar shifts in critically ill patients compared with CAVH and CAVHD. Specialist nursing and facilities needed. TPN difficult

accumulation of extracellular fluid potassium may not only be due to reduced renal clearance but can be caused by tissue necrosis, crush injury, haemolysis and acidaemia, all of which tend to release intracellular potassium into the extracellular space.

Treatment of hyperkalaemia includes reduction of potassium intake, removal of necrotic tissue and the administration of dextrose and insulin, which causes a shift of potassium from the extracellular space to the intracellular space. Ion exchange resins given enterally will reduce whole body potassium, but in the critically ill, hyperkalaemia may represent a shift of potassium into the extracellular space rather than a whole body potassium overload. Intravenous calcium administration will ameliorate the cardio-depressive effects of hyperkalaemia, but continuous arteriovenous haemofiltration (CAVH) or continous arteriovenous haemodiafiltration (CAVHD) are generally the most effective treatments for severe hyperkalaemia in acute renal failure. A summary of renal replacement therapies is given in Table 3.7.

Summary

The renal response to shock is rapid, and is directed towards retention of fluid and sodium. In severe hypovolaemia the blood supply to 'essential' organs is preserved at the expense of the renal circulation and glomerular filtration ceases. The longer renal hypoperfusion is left untreated, the greater the risk of intrinsic renal failure. Serial laboratory monitoring of renal function plays a major role in the early detection and appropriate treatment of acute renal impairment in the critically ill.

THE BRAIN

FUNCTIONS

The functions of the brain include cognition, the initiation and control of motor activity, the analysis of sensory inputs, the control of body temperature, appetite, much of the endocrine system, the autonomic nervous system, and respiration. Brain failure can affect any or all of these. Loss of, for example, cognitive, motor and sensory ('higher' functions, dependent for the greater part on the cerebrum) may be partial or complete but their complete loss is still compatible with life. The functions of the brain essential to the maintenance of homoeostasis are located in the brain stem. Cardiac function is affected by the inputs from the brain, but the heartbeat is initiated in the heart itself. However, respiratory movements are initiated and integrated by the respiratory centre in the brain stem, and if this fails, and the respiration is not maintained artificially, the patient dies.

CAUSES OF BRAIN DYSFUNCTION

Brain dysfunction may be caused by structural damage (due for example to a head injury, tumour or haemorrhage), or by a failure of supply or utilization of nutrients.

Although during starvation the brain can utilise ketones as an energy source, under normal circumstances its obligate substrate is glucose. The brain has no glycogen stores, and thus requires a continuous supply both of glucose as an energy substrate, and of oxygen for its utilization. The brain consumes some 120g glucose daily, and accounts for some 60% of the body's glucose utilization in the resting state. Even during fasting, substrate supply is dependent on a continuous blood-born supply of ketones, since the brain does not store fat, and fatty acids, which in the blood stream are bound to albumin, cannot cross the blood-brain barrier.

Any interference with the supply of glucose and oxygen to the brain, whether as a result of intracranial or extracranial conditions, may thus lead to brain dysfunction.

BRAIN DYSFUNCTION

It is necessary here to review the terminology. In its most severe manifestation, **coma** is a pathological state in which the patient is completely unaware of self and environment, even when stimulated. Patients appear to be asleep, but cannot be aroused. Coma is the opposite of consciousness, which has three components - **arousal** (the appearance of wakefulness, i.e., the eyes are open), **awareness** (which includes orientation and the ability to communicate), and appropriate **voluntary motor activity** (for example, in response to commands). Although terms including **'stupor'** and **'pre-coma'** have been used to describe patients with decreased consciousness who are not unrousable, the use of scoring systems (see below) allows more precise definitions to be made, which allow more precise monitoring of patients' mental states.

Patients do not usually remain in true coma for more than 2-4 weeks. If the causative disorder is reversible, they may recover, or progress to a **vegetative state**, in which arousal is apparent and reflex motor activity is present but there is no evidence of cognition, awareness or purposeful activity. This should be contrasted with the **locked-in syndrome**, in which patients are almost completely paralyzed, but remain conscious. Eye movements may be preserved, and afford a means for patients to communicate awareness.Vegetative state is usually due to cortical necrosis while the locked-in syndrome is usually due to extensive brain stem damage.

Table 3.8 Causes of Coma

Category	Cause	Subtype
• Structural brain damage	- Trauma	
	- Tumour	
	- Infarction	
	- Haematoma	
	- Infection	- abscess
		- meningitis
		- encephalitis
• Metabolic	- Hypoxia	
	- Hypoglycaemia	
	- Hyperosmolal states e.g., severe hyperglycaemia	
	- Hepatic, renal, pancreatic failure	
	- Nutritional disorders (e.g., thiamine deficiency)	
	- Severe electrolyte disturbances	
	- Severe hypothyroidism	
• Pharmacological	- Alcohol	
	- Sedative drugs	
	- Poisons and other drugs	
• Miscellaneous	- Post-ictal*	
	- Mild head injuries ('concussion')*	

*coma is short-lived and reversible; mechanisms are uncertain

If the cause of coma is irreversible, or even when it is not, but irreversible brain damage has occurred, death usually supervenes.

Other states of altered consciousness include **delirium**, an acute state in which the patient is fully awake but is disorientated and confused, and **dementia**, in which arousal is maintained but there is a progressive loss of mental functions, especially short term memory.

CAUSES OF COMA

There are many potential causes of coma, but they can be divided into structural, metabolic, and drug-related. Some important causes are indicated in Table 3.8.

Causes may coexist; it is particularly important to consider the possibility that coma in patients with head injuries may be in part related to alcohol.

THE ASSESSMENT OF COMA

Although from the information in Table 3.8, it will be clear that biochemical investigations may be vital in determining the cause (and thus,

Table 3.9 The Glasgow Coma scale

Response		Score
• Eye opening	- None	1
	- To pain only	2
	- To speech	3
	- Spontaneous	4
• Verbal response	- None	1
	- Incomprehensible sounds	2
	- Inappropriate words	3
	- Confused conversation	4
	- Normally orientated	5
• Motor response	- None	1
	- Abnormal extension (decerebrate rigidity)	2
	- Abnormal flexion	3
	- Withdrawal	4
	- Localized in relation to pain	5
	- Obeys commands	6

Total score thus has range 3-15; score of 8 or less indicates coma; the lower the score the deeper the coma.

to some extent, the management, of coma), they have no role in assessing severity. The most widely used method is the Glasgow coma scale, in which three indicators of consciousness – eye-opening, motor activity and verbal response are assessed and the results combined to give a numerical score (Table 3.9). A modified version has been devised for use with children. Charting the progress of coma by repeated assessment of the score is vital to the management of the comatose patient. If deterioration occurs, or a predicted improvement does not, further investigation is required to establish the cause.

THE MANAGEMENT OF COMA

Maintenance of the airway is vital. The underlying cause must be treated appropriately. Skilled nursing care to avoid skin breakdown, and physiotherapy both to the chest, to facilitate respiration and gas exchange, and to the limbs, to prevent the development of contractures, are also essential. A histamine (H_2) antagonist is often given to block gastric acid secretion with the aim of preventing stress-induced peptic ulceration. An adequate circulatory volume must be maintained, and metabolic and acid-base status monitored and any abnormalities corrected. The extent and frequency of biochemical monitoring required will depend on the nature and severity of the cause of coma. Body temperature must be maintained, and any infection treated. If coma persists for more than a few days, nutritional support, preferably enteral, will be required.

If seizures develop in a comatose patient, they must be controlled with an appropriate anticonvulsant, not only to prevent further intracranial damage, but also to prevent displacement of intravascular catheters, etc.

Monitoring of intracranial pressure may be required, particularly in patients with head injuries, following craniotomy and in metabolic encephalopathies (e.g., hepatic encephalopathy). Since the total volume of the intracranial contents is fixed by the internal dimensions of the cranium, an increase in the volume of any intracranial structure must lead to an increase in intracranial pressure (ICP), unless there is a commensurate decrease in the volume of some other structure. The normal ICP is approximately 10mmHg and values above 15-20mmHg are regarded as elevated. Persistence of the ICP above 60mmHg is almost always associated with a fatal outcome. The most dangerous adverse effects of a rise in ICP are a decrease in cerebral perfusion (which is determined by the difference between mean arterial blood pressure and ICP), and herniation of the cerebellar tonsils into the foramen magnum, with or without downward movement of the brain stem, which may both compromise the brain stem's blood supply and cause direct structural damage.

A number of techniques are available for continuous monitoring of the ICP; although an intraventricular cannula is probably the most reliable method and has the potential advantage of allowing the drainage of CSF, subdural pressure transducers are widely used. Techniques that can be used in an attempt to reduce the ICP include hyperventilation, and the administration of mannitol or dexamethasone. Hyperventilation lowers arterial PCO_2 and the consequent change in pH causes cerebral vasoconstriction and limits cerebral blood flow. Renal compensation corrects the pH within 2-3 days and cerebral blood flow returns to normal; sudden discontinuation of hyperventilation can lead to a rise in PCO_2 and in ICP. The major use of hyperventilation is in patients with head injuries. Mannitol reduces cerebral oedema (and hence ICP) through an osmotic effect; since it is excreted by the kidneys, repeated infusions are necessary to achieve a plasma osmolality in the range 300-320mmol/kg. Corticosteroids reduce oedema by a direct effect and are particularly useful in patients with cerebral tumours.

PROGNOSIS AND RECOVERY

The prognosis in coma depends to a considerable extent on the nature and severity of the underlying cause. When coma is due to metabolic causes or drugs, recovery may be complete; it is less likely to be so when there is structural damage although this will depend on the site and extent of damage. It is essential that every effort is made to prevent secondary hypoxic damage, since this can considerably worsen an initially favourable prognosis.

The first sign of recovery from coma is usually opening of the eyes, followed by speaking a few words and response to commands. A period of confusion and disinhibited behaviour may follow, and then a period of quiet confusion. Amnesia is typical during this time; the duration of amnesia is a useful guide to the severity of diffuse brain damage, especially after head injury.

METABOLIC CONSEQUENCES OF CEREBRAL DYSFUNCTION

In addition to metabolic disorders being a *cause* of cerebral dysfunction, metabolic disturbances can also *arise* in patients with cerebral dysfunction. Head injury can cause pituitary stalk section, producing pan-hypopituitarism. The diabetes insipidus that develops may only be temporary or partial, since vasopressin can be secreted directly from the hypothalamus. Injury to the brain, and many other intracerebral conditions, for example, tumours or abcesses, can cause the syndrome of inappropriate antidiuresis (SIAD).

BIOCHEMICAL ASSESSMENT OF CEREBRAL DYSFUNCTION

Although biochemical tests are vital in the management of patients with cerebral dysfunction and may help to establish a cause, they provide virtually no information on its severity nor its prognosis. This contrasts with the use of biochemical tests in patients with, for example, renal or hepatic failure. Although the brain is metabolically very active, this activity of the brain is not reflected in the blood. Examination of cerebrospinal fluid (CSF) (if such fluid can be obtained safely) may help in establishing the cause of cerebral dysfunction, particularly if this is of primary intracranial origin (e.g., the presence of blood following a subarachnoid haemorrhage or the typical changes seen in bacterial infection); with cerebral dysfunction secondary to other conditions, examination of the CSF, though it may reveal relatively specific abnormalities (e.g., a high glutamine in hepatic encephalopathy) is not of diagnostic value.

Measurements of brain-derived materials, (e.g., the BB isoenzyme of creatine kinase) in peripheral blood have been studied in relation to the diagnosis of brain injury but are of no value, presumably because their access to the circulation is impeded by the blood-brain barrier. The continuing rapid evolution of high-resolution imaging techniques provides far more sensitive and specific means of assessing brain damage.

BRAIN DEATH

The increasing success of cadaver organ transplantation for the treatment not only of renal but also hepatic, cardiac and pulmonary failure, has made it essential to lay down strict criteria for the diagnosis of brain death, that is, brain damage so severe that there is no detectable brain function even though the heart continues to beat. Even when organs cannot be harvested for transplantation, this diagnosis recognizes that recovery will not occur and allows the withdrawal of respiratory support so that nature can take its course.

The minimum criteria for the diagnosis of brain death are:

- positively diagnosed structural brain damage
- irreversibility of the underlying cause of the damage
- loss of brain stem function.

It is inappropriate to discuss this subject in detail here, but in essence the brain dead patient will be in coma, with no discernible cerebral response to any stimulus. Eye movements will be absent, corneal, pharyngeal and laryngeal reflexes absent and the patient will be apnoeic. In practice, many patients in whom the diagnosis is considered will be on ventilatory support. A complete absence of respiratory effort must be confirmed. Oxygenation must be maintained by delivery of adequate (6 L/min) oxygen through the endotracheal tube and sufficient time elapse to allow the PCO_2 to rise to a sufficient level (6.6 kPa) to act as a respiratory stimulant.

Biochemical tests are essential to the diagnosis of brain death. Potentially reversible metabolic and pharmacological conditions which can cause coma must be excluded. In particular, it may be necessary to measure the plasma concentrations of sedative drugs which may have been used therapeutically or drugs which may have been present in the body on admission to hospital (including alcohol and drugs of abuse). Brain death should not be diagnosed while such drugs are still detectable in the plasma.

THE LIVER

FUNCTIONS

The liver has a major role in the processing of energy substrates. It is responsible for the storage of glucose as glycogen and for the production of glucose by gluconeogenesis and glycogenolysis; it can synthesize fatty acids from glucose and convert these and free fatty acids derived from the blood into triacylglycerols (triglycerides) which are exported to be stored or used as energy substrates. Fatty acids can also be converted to ketones, another important energy substrate. The liver is a major site of lipoprotein metabolism, and is responsible for production of bile and the excretion of cholesterol and bilirubin. It is also capable of detoxifying a wide variety of drugs and other foreign compounds and has an important physiological role in the metabolism of hormones. It is an important site of amino acid metabolism, is the major organ of ureagenesis and thus has a role in hydrogen ion homeostasis. It is responsible for the synthesis of many plasma proteins (other than immunoglobulins), including albumin, protease inhibitors, transport proteins and the coagulation factors.

The liver has considerable reserve capacity, and the removal of up to about 90% is compatible with life. Furthermore, it has a remarkable capacity for regeneration, and following partial surgical resection or even severe hepatic necrosis, provided that sufficient functioning hepatic tissue is left to maintain homoeostasis in the short term, the liver will usually regenerate and regain its original weight.

The liver has a dual blood supply, receiving arterial blood through the hepatic artery, and partially deoxygenated blood (approx 60% saturated) through the portal vein. The blood flow through the liver is approximately 25% of the cardiac output at rest. Only about 30% of this is through the hepatic artery, the remainder being through the portal vein; as a result, approximately equal quantities of oxygen are derived from each source. The liver comprises some 100 000 functional units (acini). Each acinus has a vascular stalk. Hepatocytes nearest the centre of the acinus (zone 1) are least susceptible to hypoxia; those at the periphery, clustered around the hepatic venule (centrilobular, zone 3) are the most susceptible.

LIVER DYSFUNCTION

Life-threatening liver failure can develop in patients with previously normal hepatic function, particularly following damage induced by drugs or toxins, for example, paracetamol taken in overdose, or viral infection such as hepatitis B or C. Liver failure can also occur in patients with existing liver disease, if the function of the organ is further compromised, for example if a patient with cirrhosis sustains a gastrointestinal haemorrhage.

Shock liver - acute hepatic dysfunction related to hypoperfusion - is a well recognized consequence of acute hypotension of any cause. Evidence of less severe hepatic impairment is also frequently present in patients with chronic cardiac failure.

Only **acute hepatic failure** - by definition, severe hepatic dysfunction occurring within six months of the first onset of liver disease in a previously healthy liver - will be considered further in detail here. The discussion is mainly devoted to the metabolic aspects and the role of the laboratory in the management of patients with liver failure. Readers seeking more information on the clinical aspects should consult references indicated at the end of the section.

SHOCK LIVER

The liver injury in this condition results from hypotension, for example due to haemorrhage, burns, sepsis or acute heart failure (coronary thrombosis, pulmonary embolism). There is often pre-existing cardiac disease and the condition can sometimes occur in congestive cardiac failure. It is frequently seen in association with dysfunction of other organs, as part of the syndrome of multiple organ failure.

The presentation and severity are variable, ranging from the isolated finding of very high plasma aminotransferase activities to fulminant hepatic failure. The likelihood of fulminant hepatic failure is greater if there is pre-existing chronic cardiac failure. Otherwise, the severity of the changes is related to the duration of shock rather than to its cause: shock lasting for less than ten hours rarely causes liver cell necrosis whereas if it persists for more than 24 hours, hepatic necrosis is invariable.

Aminotransferase activities frequently rise to ten times, and exceptionally to as high as one hundred times the upper limit of the reference ranges within 24 hours, falling rapidly if there is a rapid improvement in cardiovascular state. Plasma bilirubin concentration and alkaline phosphatase activity do not usually rise to more than 2-4 times the upper limits of their reference ranges; the prothrombin time is only slightly prolonged unless fulminant hepatic failure develops. Shock liver does not itself cause a fall in plasma albumin concentration, though this may be low for other reasons (e.g., sepsis).

Injury to hepatocytes in shock liver is primarily due to hepatic hypoxia as a result of impaired perfusion. Hypotension leads to intense angiotensin II-mediated splanchnic vasoconstriction. Absorption of endotoxin from the gut may also play a part in the development of the syndrome. The brunt of the damage is born by the centrilobular (zone 3) hepatocytes. Interestingly, much of the tissue damage is thought to develop during reperfusion, as a result of the generation of oxygen-derived free radicals, and scavengers of free radicals may have a part to play in the management of this condition.

The outcome of shock liver depends almost entirely on the severity of the underlying cardiovascular dysfunction.

FULMINANT HEPATIC FAILURE

The term 'fulminant hepatic failure' is widely used to refer to acute liver failure complicated by hepatic encephalopathy (cerebral dysfunction, particularly clouding of consciousness) developing within eight weeks of the first symptom. Liver cell damage leads to jaundice and a bleeding tendency (due to decreased synthesis of coagulation factors) but many of the clinical features are non-specific.

Fulminant hepatic failure, as its name implies, is a condition of the utmost severity, but in those who survive, there are no long-term hepatic sequelae. In the United Kingdom, the commonest causes are paracetamol overdose and viral hepatitis (particularly types B and 'non-A, non-B'). Other causes include drugs, Wilson's disease, other viruses and poisons, cardiogenic shock (particularly in patients with underlying cardiac disease) and shock from other causes.

Clinical manifestations

Jaundice usually precedes the onset of encephalopathy, the first manifestation of which (Grade 1) is usually asterixis - a failure of the ability to sustain a fixed posture (e.g., with arms and fingers extended and the wrists dorsiflexed: 'liver flap'). Table 3.10 indicates the principal features of more severe grades of encephalopathy. Cerebral oedema is present in approximately 80% of patients at autopsy. In life, it may be suggested by the presence of decerebrate posturing and abnormalities of brain stem function. In the early stages, vomiting is common although abdominal pain is infrequent; other non-specific features, e.g., tachycardia, hypotension, hyperventilation and fever may develop. Fulminant hepatic failure of whatever cause is frequently complicated by renal failure ('pre-renal', intrinsic or 'functional' {see below}). Uncontrollable bleeding is a frequent terminal event.

Table 3.10 Grades of hepatic encephalopathy

Grade	Features
1	Asterixis
2	Confusion, drowsiness, agitation, behaviour disturbance
3	Stupor with phases of agitation, severe confusion
4	Coma

MANAGEMENT

The management is primarily supportive; the liver has considerable regenerative powers and if vital functions can be maintained, complete recovery may occur. There is no evidence from controlled trials that measures designed to remove toxins, for example charcoal haemoperfusion, result in any sustained benefit. The only curative treatment is hepatic transplantation.

Supportive measures include maintenance of an adequate cardiac output and gas exchange, fluid, electrolyte, acid-base, and nutrient status; appropriate management of any coagulopathy; renal replacement therapy (e.g., haemodialysis or filtration); prevention or early treatment of cerebral oedema (with intravenous mannitol and, if the urine flow rate is poor, haemofiltration); prevention or treatment of any infection, etc. Avoidance of potentially hepatotoxic, nephrotoxic and sedative drugs is essential.

The survival rate of patients with fulminant hepatic failure who do not progress beyond Grades 1 & 2 coma is approximately 66%, but even with the best supportive care, the overall survival of patients with Grade 4 encephalopathy is only of the order of 20-30%. Overall, it is better for patients with paracetamol overdose than for those with viral or drug-related hepatitis, and in the viral group, better for hepatitis A related disease than for B and 'non-A, non-B'.

Although liver transplantation is potentially curative, since the procedure involves the removal of the patient's own liver, it must be reserved for those who would otherwise be expected to die. It is therefore essential to have reliable prognostic criteria on which to base a decision to proceed to transplantation. The major adverse factors are: grade 3 or 4 coma, arterial hydrogen ion concentration >50nmol/L (pH<7.3), prothrombin time >100s and plasma creatinine concentration >300μmol/L. Recently, measurements of coagulation factors have been shown to be valuable prognostic indicators, a ratio of (factor V/factor VIII) >30 being associated with a very small chance of survival in fulminant hepatic failure without transplantation. Survival figures for transplanted patients continue to improve, with more than 60% survival with follow-up for up to three years being usual.

METABOLIC DERANGEMENTS AND LABORATORY MONITORING

The laboratory has an important part to play in the management of fulminant hepatic failure, in determining the cause, monitoring progress, detecting complications and indicating the prognosis. Measurement of the plasma paracetamol concentration is essential to the rational use of its antidote, N-acetylcysteine. Wilson's disease should always be excluded in patients under the age of 35 by measurements of plasma copper and caeruloplasmin. Serological tests for a viral aetiology can be misleading since hepatitis B surface antigen may have been cleared before the patient is admitted (a good prognostic feature in hepatitis B infection) and antibody may not have become detectable. The metabolic features and complications of fulminant hepatic failure are summarized in Table 3.11.

'LIVER FUNCTION' TESTS

Derangements of these tests are universally present. They include an increase in plasma bilirubin concentration and increases, sometimes

Table 3.11 Laboratory features and complications of fulminant hepatic failure

'Liver function' tests	
• bilirubin	high
• aminotransferases	very high (but can fall with massive liver damage)
• gamma-glutamyl transferase	high
• albumin	normal (unless low for other reasons; but may fall later)
'Electrolytes'	
• sodium	low
• potassium	low (may be increased in renal failure)
• phosphate	low (may be increased in renal failure)
Renal function tests	
• creatinine	high
• urea	may be elevated; can be normal or even low
Acid-base	
• hydrogen ion	usually low (respiratory ± metabolic alkalosis)
Glucose	low
Coagulation indices	
• prothrombin	time prolonged
• factors II, V*, VII, IX, X	low
• factor VIII	may be increased

*particularly

massive, in plasma aminotransferase activities. Serial measurements of bilirubin are of value in assessing progress but aminotransferases are unhelpful; their activities may fall if the patient's condition deteriorates. Plasma albumin concentration is usually normal initially but tends to fall later, in part reflecting decreased synthetic capacity.

Nitrogen metabolism

Impairment of hepatic nitrogen metabolism leads to decreased ureagenesis with low plasma urea concentrations (unless renal failure develops, see below); blood ammonium concentrations are increased but they correlate neither with the depth of coma nor the prognosis. There is a characteristic imbalance in plasma amino acid concentrations, with increases in the aromatic amino acids and methionine, and decreases in the branched chain amino acids. Despite much work on the subject, there is no proven role for infusion of branched chain amino acids in fulminant hepatic failure.

Acid-base status

The characteristic acid-base disturbance is a respiratory alkalosis, due to central stimulation of respiration; it tends to be present early, but later, respiratory depression may contribute to an acidosis. Vomiting, nasogastric aspiration and hypokalaemia may all contribute to a metabolic alkalosis but the development of renal failure may lead to a metabolic acidosis. The presence of acidosis is a poor prognostic feature. As a result of decreased hepatic lactate metabolism, hyperlactataemia is frequently present but the plasma lactate concentration correlates poorly with the hydrogen ion concentration, presumably because of the multiplicity of other factors affecting this.

Water and mineral metabolism

Water retention with hyponatraemia is common and multifactorial; potassium depletion, due to gastrointestinal loss, alkalosis and possibly decreased hepatic metabolism of aldosterone, leads to hypokalaemia but hyperkalaemia may develop if there is renal failure. Hypophosphataemia, which may be severe, is frequently present in patients with fulminant hepatic failure, more so when this is related to paracetamol poisoning. The mechanisms include intracellular trapping of phosphate as a result of dextrose infusion and alkalosis, and excessive renal excretion. Hypophosphataemia should be actively sought and corrected in patients with fulminant hepatic failure since it has a number of adverse effects, including impairment of respiratory function. Whether it contributes to the development of encephalopathy is uncertain.

Renal function

Renal failure is a frequent complication of fulminant hepatic failure and imposes a poor prognosis. It is usually either functional in origin or due to acute tubular necrosis. Functional renal failure is a form of renal failure in which, despite a normal (or even increased) cardiac output, there is a reduction in renal blood flow and glomerular filtration rate which lead to oliguria without any histological evidence of renal damage. It appears to be due to changes in intrarenal blood flow, with an increase in pre-glomerular vascular resistance leading to impaired glomerular perfusion and diversion of blood away from the cortex. The pathogenesis is complex, but contributory factors include changes in renal prostanoid metabolism, hyperreninaemia and stimulation of the sympathetic nervous system. The reader wishing to learn more should consult the references cited at the end of this chapter.

Because of the decreased hepatic ureagenesis, plasma urea concentration is a poor guide to renal function although it does usually increase if renal failure develops. Plasma creatinine, which is independent of hepatic function, is a better reflection of renal function, and should be used to guide therapeutic decisions, e.g., when to initiate dialysis. However, it should be remembered that plasma creatinine measurements made using some methods may be unreliable (giving falsely low results) when hyperbilirubinaemia is present.

Glucose and fat metabolism

Other metabolic abnormalities which can be related directly to hepatic dysfunction include hypoglycaemia (due to impaired gluconeogenesis and exhaustion/destruction of hepatic glycogen reserves), and a low plasma cholesterol concentration. Plasma free fatty acid concentrations are usually elevated, perhaps reflecting decreased hepatic ketogenesis. To prevent hypoglycaemia, dextrose should be infused continuously (with potassium unless there is renal failure) and the blood glucose concentration checked frequently. Water soluble vitamins must also be given since hepatic stores may be depleted, although they may not be normally metabolised to their active forms. If enteral nutritional support is impossible, total parenteral nutrition may be required.

COAGULATION DEFECTS

Evidence of coagulopathy is invariably present in patients with fulminant hepatic failure. Uncontrollable bleeding is a common terminal event. It is due primarily to decreased hepatic synthesis of clotting factors, although other factors, e.g., thrombocytopaenia and low-grade disseminated intravascular coagulation may be contributory. The prothrombin time (International Normalised Ratio (INR)) is markedly prolonged and not significantly corrected by parenteral vitamin K. Levels of factors II, V (particularly), VII, IX and X are often reduced to below 50% of normal although the concentration of factor VIII may be increased. The prognostic significance of these changes has been referred to above. An increase in the concentration of factor V may be the earliest sign of impending recovery.

THE GUT

Over the past fifteen years, organ failure in the critically ill has been described as 'sequential organ failure', 'sepsis syndrome' or 'multiple organ failure'. Many of the features of multiple organ failure are similar to those seen in severe sepsis but without any evidence of a source of infection. Organs remote from the primary disease frequently fail, and organ failure occurs days or even weeks after the initiating condition. Many mechanisms which might be implicated in delayed and widespread organ damage in the critically ill have been studied and the reader is referred to references at the end of this chapter. However there is increasing evidence linking gut ischaemia to acute lung injury and multiple organ failure. In shock, the blood flow to the gut is reduced due to vasoconstriction or low cardiac output or both, preserving blood supply to 'essential' organs. Progressive gut failure following shock may allow translocation of bacteria and bacterial toxins from the lumen of the gut into the circulation, and contribute or cause remote organ damage, in particular the lung.

The intestinal mucosa forms a barrier between the intestinal lumen and the blood stream. The gut contains bacteria and bacterial toxins together with potentially harmful enteric secretions such as hydrochloric acid and enzymes, and yet it also contains nutrients which must be absorbed. The absorption of nutrients must take place selectively. There are bacterial, mechanical, immunological and hepatic mechanisms summarised below which prevent the passage of deleterious agents into the systemic circulation.

The normal obligate anaerobic intestinal flora are closely associated with the intestinal mucosa and outnumber potentially pathogenic enteric aerobic bacteria in the order of 1000-10,000 to 1. They compete for nutrients and form a barrier preventing pathogens reaching the mucosa. This barrier is lost when broad spectrum antibiotics are given since the obligate anaerobes are generally more sensitive to antibiotics than the rest of the intestinal flora.

In the healthy gut, peristalsis prevents prolonged contact of bacteria with the mucosal wall and reduces the possibility of organisms penetrating the mucosal layer and reaching the epithelium. If peristalsis stops due to, for example, an ileus or obstruction, bacterial stasis will occur and there will be a greater risk of bacteria traversing the intestinal epithelium.

The constant desquamation of epithelial cells from the villous tips and their replacement every few days by cells migrating from the intestinal crypts, also reduces the possibility of any bacteria which have reached the epithelial cells, entering the systemic circulation. Prolonged interruption of this regenerative process due to shock will cause villous atrophy and allow bacterial contamination of the circulation.

Lymphocytes and macrophages are found in association with epithelial cells, the lamina propria and mesenteric lymph nodes and can regulate the local immune response to oral antigens and intestinal bacteria. Secretory IgA produced by primed B cells within the intestinal mucosa selectively bind bacteria within the lumen and prevent them adhering to the mucosal wall.

Bacteria and endotoxins which reach the portal blood stream are normally inactivated by the reticuloendothelial system in the liver. Thus provided intestinal and hepatic function are intact, the 'septic threat' of the gut is minimised.

If gut ischaemia is severe, then the protective mechanism described above will be compromised, resulting in increased gut permeability to bacteria and toxins which may overwhelm the hepatic reticuloendothelial system and lead to systemic endotoxinaemia. Shock can also lead to gut failure, ranging from an inability to absorb enteral feeds, to major structural failure such as perforation or necrosis both of which are likely to be fatal unless treated promptly. Within the stomach, ischaemia can lead to stress ulceration and gastric bleeding.

Management of intestinal function in the critically ill is directed towards preserving gut function, thus providing not only a route for the maintenance of nutrition, but also preserving the gut mucosal barrier. Assessment of gut perfusion during surgical procedures can be made using gastric or colonic tonometer. The tonometer measures intraluminal pH which reflects mucosal oxygen delivery. However, post-operative monitoring of gut perfusion by tonometry is not routinely performed, and functional adequacy of the gut is generally assessed by absorption of nasogastric feed.

Stress ulceration can be prevented by inhibiting gastric acid production with H_2 receptor antagonists, or by administration of antacids. However, this carries the risk of bacterial infestation of the normally sterile stomach and migration of bacteria to the oesophagus and aspiration into the lungs causing pneumonia. Sucralfate is effective in preventing stress bleeding and reduces the risk of pneumonia, but can congeal in the stomach and cause obstruction.

Enteral feeding is preferred to TPN wherever possible because it is technically easier and carries less risk. The intestinal mucosa obtains significant amounts of substrate from the gut lumen, thus even small amounts of feed help provide nourishment. *In vivo* and *in vitro* studies suggest that the mucosa requires specific intraluminal substrates such as glutamine and that, in contrast to other tissues, glucose and free fatty acids contribute little to the energy needs of the intestine. Clinical studies have demonstrated increased survival rates, lower infection rates, improved immune function and maintenance of mucosal mass in patients fed enterally. For this reason, even in patients with gut failure whose major route for feeding parenteral, a 'trickle' of enteral nutrition is desirable and should be attempted.

Preservation of gastrointestinal function in the critically ill can no longer be viewed as simply desirable for patient nutrition. Increasing evidence suggests that gastrointestinal failure not only closes an avenue for nutrition but may also initiate or perpetuate mechanisms leading to remote organ failure and death.

THE NERVOUS SYSTEM

The autonomic nervous system regulates activities of the body which are not generally under voluntary control. Homeostatic functions such as respiration, circulation, digestion, body temperature regulation, metabolism, etc., are all regulated in part by the autonomic nervous system. This system has two distinct components, the sympathetic and parasympathetic. Sympathetic nerve fibres extend to a widely distributed motor system reaching the viscera, skeletal muscle and skin. Parasympathetic nerve fibres are less widely distributed and control the activities of individual organs. In both systems, acetylcholine acts as a preganglionic neurotransmitter but there are differences in the postganglionic neurotransmitters.

The term 'adrenergic' is used for those parts of the sympathetic nervous system for which the neurotransmitters are derived from adrenaline precursors. Noradrenaline is the transmitter for most postganglionic sympathetic nerve fibres and dopamine the transmitter of the extrapyramidal system. The postganglionic neurotransmitter for the majority of parasympathetic nerve fibres is acetylcholine (cholinergic).

Since the parasympathetic nervous system controls individual organ functions such as urinary bladder emptying, motility of the gastrointestinal tract and contraction of ciliary and iris sphyncter muscles of the eye; in shock, there would be no benefit if all parasympathetic nerves discharged simultaneously. In contrast, the sympathetic nervous system in shock is activated as a single unit, resulting in co-ordinated responses. For example, sympathetic nerve impulses produce an increase in heart rate (so tending to increase cardiac output), vasoconstriction (increasing or maintaining blood pressure), bronchiolar dilatation (promoting gas exchange), redirect blood from splanchnic

Table 3.12 Summary of the effect of autonomic nerve stimulation

Tissue	Receptor	Adrenergic responses	Cholinergic responses
HEART	β-1	Inotropic and chronotropic effect	Decreased inotropic and chronotropic effect
ARTERIOLES			
• Skin & mucosa	α-1, α-2	Vasoconstriction	
	β	Vasodilatation	
• Coronary	α-1, α-2	Vasoconstriction	
	β	Vasodilatation	
• Skeletal muscle	β	Vasoconstriction	
	β-2	Vasodilatation	
• Viscera	α-1	Vasoconstriction	
	β-2	Vasodilatation	
• Renal	α-1, α-2	Vasoconstriction	
	β-1, β-2	Vasodilatation	
• Salivary gland	α-1, α-2	Vasoconstriction	Dilatation
LIVER	α-1	Glycogenolysis and gluconeogenesis	
PANCREAS			
• Acini	α, β-2	Decreased secretion	Stimulates secretion
• Islets	α-2	Decreased secretion	
	β-2	Increased secretion	
LUNG			
• Bronchial muscle	β-2	Relaxation	Contraction
GI TRACT	α-1, α-2 β-1, β-2	Generally decreased motility	Stimulates motility
NEUROHYPOPHYSIS	β-1	Vasopressin release	
ADIPOCYTES	α, β-1	Lipolysis	
SKELETAL MUSCLE	β-2	Increased contractility, glycogenolysis and potassium uptake	

and skin vascular beds to skeletal muscle (fight or flight reaction), and influenced cellular metabolism leading to mobilisation of glucose (see Chapter 2). These responses are directed to the maintenance of substrate delivery to 'essential organs'. Many of these effects are primarily mediated, or reinforced by, adrenaline secreted from the adrenal medulla.

Experimental studies which showed that the same neurotransmitter agonist could produce different responses in different tissues, led to the concept of α and β receptors, stimulation of which can produce different tissues responses. As these effects became better understood, receptors have been subdivided further into β1 and β-2 and α-1 and α-2. Table 3.12 summarises some of the main tissue receptors and the effects of adrenergic and cholinergic agonists. It will be seen that cholinergic impulses by the parasympathetic nervous system frequently produce opposing effects to the adrenergic responses in individual organs.

The net result of adrenergic receptor stimulation is a series of appropriate cardiovascular and metabolic responses to shock. Table 3.13 summarises the various receptors, agonists, antagonists and the effects on tissues of receptor activation. Pharmacological modulation of these mechanisms in the critically ill will be discussed briefly.

USE OF ADRENERGIC AGONISTS IN SHOCK

Treatment of shock is aimed at optimising substrate delivery for which restoration of blood volume is essential. Assessment of the adequacy of resuscitation often involves monitoring haemodynamic parameters such as blood pressure, central venous pressure and urine output. If, despite

Table 3.13 Summary of adrenergic receptors their agonists and antagonists

Receptor	Endogenous agonists	Synthetic agonists	Antagonists
α-1	Adrenaline ⩾ Noradrenaline	Phenylephrine	Prazosin
α-2	Adrenaline ⩾ Noradrenaline	Clonidine	Yohimbine
β-1	Adrenaline = Noradenaline	Dobutamine	Metoprolol
β-2	Adrenaline	Terbutaline	

>Indicates ranking of effect

adequate restoration of blood volume, these parameters indicate persistent tissue underperfusion, then it may be necessary to use vasoactive and inotropic agents. This needs to be done with care. Clearly, administration of vasoconstricting agents in an attempt to treat shock-induced hypotension in a hypovolaemic patient may worsen tissue perfusion and substrate delivery rather than improve it.

In general, α-adrenergic agonists tend to stimulate vascular smooth muscle contraction which increase peripheral vascular resistance and blood pressure, while β-adrenergic agonists increase myocardial contraction (inotropic effect) and heart rate (chronotropic effect).

β-1 agonists such as dobutamine produce cardiac inotropic and chronotropic effects. Low doses of dopamine stimulate receptors in the renal and splanchnic vasculature producing vasodilatation and are used to preserve renal blood flow and maintain urine output in patients with oliguria. At higher doses, dopamine stimulates α-1 adrenergic receptors in vascular smooth muscle producing vasoconstriction. The uses of some common adrenergic agonists are summarised in Table 3.14. Agents which block β–adrenergic receptors are of benefit in reducing mortality and reinfarction rate in patients suffering myocardial infarction.

Table 3.14 Summary of the uses of adrenergic agonists

Agonist	Receptors	Clinical Uses
Adrenaline	β-2	Relief of bronchospasm
	α-1	Vasoconstriction to increase blood pressure or reduce bleeding locally
	β-1	Increased myocardial contraction
Noradrenaline	α-1, α-2	Short acting vasoconstriction
Dopamine (low dose)	β-1, β-2	Renal vasodilatation in oliguria
Dopamine (high dose)	β-1	Cardiac inotrope, used, for example in septic and cardiogenic shock
Dobutamine	β-1	Inotropic and chronotropic cardiac effects

* In many cases more selective β and α receptor agonists are now available

ENDOCRINE SYSTEM

Endocrine responses in shock are directed towards restoration and preservation of homeostasis by maintaining delivery of substrates to the tissues. Understanding the endocrine response to shock allows resuscitation to augment homeostatic mechanisms and avoid the misdiagnosis of a primary endocrine disorder when the disorder is in fact secondary to the shock-induced condition. The principle hormones influencing metabolism have been described in Chapter 2.

PITUITARY

Hormones from both the anterior and posterior pituitary are released in response to shock, generally secondarily to increased secretion of hypothalamic releasing hormones or decreased secretion of pituitary-inhibiting peptides. Vasopressin (antidiuretic hormone) is released from the posterior pituitary in shock in response to hypovolaemia and increased plasma osmolality, and has both vasoconstrictor and water retaining actions. Circulating growth hormone concentrations are increased in patients with shock and remain persistently high in patients with burn injury, but the purpose of this is unclear. In normal subjects, growth hormone mobilises free fatty acids, decreases glucose uptake by tissues and increases hepatic glucose output. However, the relative contribution of growth hormone to shock-induced insulin resistance is not well defined. Soldiers on combat duty showed increased circulating growth hormone concentrations, which rose further following injury, decreased in those who recovered, but remained elevated in those who died. Prolactin is also released from the anterior pituitary in shock but the advantages of this, if any, also remains unclear.

Hypothalamic corticotrophin releasing hormone stimulates adrenocorticotrophic hormone (ACTH) release from the anterior pituitary in shock together with β-endorphin, both of which are derived from a common precursor (pro-opiomelanocortin). ACTH stimulates adrenal cortisol release, while β-endorphin may play a role in stress-induced analgesia, which was first described in the severely wounded during the Second World War.

Thyroid stimulated hormone (TSH) is released from the anterior pituitary in response to hypothalamic thyrotrophin releasing hormone (TRH).

Basal plasma TSH concentrations can be normal, high or low in the critically ill, and the response to TRH administration is frequently subnormal. Recent studies of patients in intensive care units have shown a strong inverse correlation between plasma TSH concentration and survival. Opioid peptides, cortisol, dopamine and growth hormone all inhibit TSH release, and this may explain the association between TSH suppression, disease severity and mortality.

ADRENALS

Except in patients with primary adrenal disease, the adrenal medulla and cortex function at increased levels of activity in shock. Adrenaline is the major catecholamine secreted by the adrenal medulla, while noradrenaline in mostly derived from sympathetic neural end plates. Adrenaline is released within 5-60 minutes of the shock-inducing stimulus whilst circulating noradrenaline concentrations rise more slowly. In addition to their metabolic actions, of increasing circulating glucose concentrations by inhibiting insulin secretion and stimulating pancreatic glucagon release (Chapter 2), adrenaline and noradrenaline stimulate β-1 receptors in the heart, increasing myocardial contractility (inotropic effect), heart rate (chronotropic effect) and stimulate α-1 receptors producing vasoconstriction of selected vascular beds (e.g., gut, skin and skeletal muscle) thus tending to preserve perfusion of 'essential organs' (See page 105).

Circulating concentrations of catecholamines remain high during shock, fall in response to correction of hypovolaemia, but only return to normal on recovery when normal tissue perfusion has been restored. Catecholamine mediated (sympathetic) responsiveness to shock is depressed by some anaesthetic agents (especially barbiturates and by spinal anaesthesia). Barbiturates reduce sympathetic nerve activity, and in shock can cause hypotension, circulatory collapse and cardiac arrest. Spinal anaesthesia involves injection of local anaesthetic into the lumbar subarachnoid space. Arteries and arterioles dilate in sympathetically innervated areas reducing peripheral vascular resistance and mean arterial blood pressure.

Theoretically, since epidural anaesthesia (injection of local anaesthetic into the epidural space) is not associated with direct sympathetic blockade as in spinal anaesthesia, the cardiovascular effects would be expected to be less. However in practice, since larger doses of anaesthetic are used in epidural anaesthesia, and concentrations in the blood are higher, the cardiovascular responses are similar to those in spinal anaesthesia. Thus the normal catecholamine-mediated cardiovascular response to hypovolaemia, which is essential for survival in shock, may be inadequate during anaesthesia and for this reason it is essential that hypovolaemia is corrected prior to anaesthesia. A number of studies have demonstrated that epidural anaesthesia or large doses of opiates depress the 'stress' response to surgery including a significant (but not dangerous) reduction in cortisol release. Maintenance of epidural anaesthesia into the post-operative period reduces negative nitrogen balance and improves respiratory function.

Elevated serum cortisol concentrations in response to pituitary ACTH release are always found in shock except in patients with adrenal failure. Thus in the critically ill, circulating cortisol concentrations within the reference range are abnormal and suggest adrenal insufficiency. Adequate cortisol release is essential for the survival of the critically ill, and patients with depressed adrenal function due, for example, to disease or long term steroid administration, will require appropriate steroid replacement, frequently in supranormal amounts.

Aldosterone is released from the adrenal zona glomerulosa in response to increased circulating angiotensin II concentrations and mediates sodium retention in shock (the release of atrial natriuretic peptide from the cardiac atria tends to be inhibited in shock, which also enhances sodium retention.) Vasoconstriction and sodium retention with attendant water conservation help to correct a hypovolaemic state.

THYROID

Thyroid hormones play a major role in cellular metabolism and are essential for the normal function of many organs. The pattern of thyroid hormone release in shock is very variable and must be interpreted with caution in the critically ill. As described above TSH secretion tends to be depressed in shock. Thyroxine (T4) is the precursor of triiodothyronine (T3) which is the biologically active hormone, 80% being derived from peripheral deiodination of T4, the remainder being secreted directly by the thyroid. In shock, peripheral conversion of T4 to T3 is reduced and increased amounts of the inactive isomeric derivative reverse T3 are formed. In shock, plasma concentrations of both T4 and T3 may be normal, low or high and do not reflect thyroidal status for several reasons.

Approximately 99.9% of thyroid hormones are bound to thyroid hormone binding globulin (TBG), albumin, and prealbumin. Inhibitors capable of blocking thyroid hormone binding have been found in the plasma in severe illness, and may increase the relative concentrations of circulating free T3 and free T4. However, low serum free T3 concentrations have been found in up to 70% of hospitalised patients, which may be due to increased conversion of T4 to the inactive reverse T3. Despite these apparent thyroidal abnormalities the vast majority of patients in intensive care units are euthyroid. Clearly attempts to evaluate thyroid status in the critically ill should be postponed until recovery in all but the rare patient admitted to the ITU with a life threatening thyroid disorder.

ENDOCRINE PANCREAS

In the early stages of shock, insulin release from the β–cells of the islets of Langerhans is suppressed, probably due in part to the insulin suppressing properties of high concentrations of catecholamines in the circulation. At a later stage of shock, plasma insulin concentrations are frequently above normal despite hyperglycaemia, indicating some form of insulin resistance. Animals studies of shock have shown similar intracellular and extra cellular glucose concentrations with hyperinsulinaemia, suggesting that insulin resistance occurs at the stage of intracellular glucose metabolism and not at the stage of glucose uptake by the cell. Pancreatic glucagon is produced by the α2 cells of the islets of Langerhans, and promotes metabolic effects which are counter-regulatory to those of insulin. Glucagon induces gluconeogenesis and glycogenolysis and, together with catecholamines, maintains glucose concentrations. Glucagon release in shock is mediated by both sympathetic and parasympathetic systems and can be blocked by propranolol. It has been proposed that when the molar insulin / glucagon ratio exceeds five, anabolism and protein conservation supervenes, but ratios of less than three are associated with glycogenolysis, gluconeogenesis and proteolysis.

TISSUE MEDIATORS

Although not emanating from a specific endocrine organ, a variety of mediators are released into the circulation from injured, infected or ischaemic tissues which have both secreting cell (autocrine), local (paracrine), and remote (endocrine) effects. This is a rapidly expanding field of knowledge, detailed consideration of which is beyond the scope of this text. However some of the more well understood classes of mediators are described briefly below.

CYTOKINES

Cytokines are a family of proteins and glycoproteins produced by a variety of cells including leucocytes both in membrane-bound forms and secreted directly into the circulation. Tumour necrosis factor (TNF) is a cytokine which has received a great deal of attention. It is produced by neutrophils, activated lymphocytes, macrophages and a variety of other cells including smooth muscle cells and vascular endothelium. Together with interleukin 1, TNF may have a primary role in initiating the release of a cascade of cytokines and other factors associated with inflammatory processes.

Early work demonstrated that the inflammatory effects of endotoxin were mediated by TNF. Receptors for TNF are ubiquitous and the effects of TNF at the cellular level are similar to those seen following tissue injury. These include induction of neutrophil degranulation, lysozyme release, oxygen derived free radical generation and neutrophil adherence to vascular endothelium. Interleukin 1 is also produced by macrophages in response to endotoxins and infection and induces hepatic acute phase protein synthesis, fever, release of corticotrophin releasing hormone and thus ACTH-mediated adrenal steroidogenesis. Interleukin 6 is also produced by a wide range of cell types including macrophages, monocytes, fibroblasts and vascular endothelial cells. The actions of interleukin 6 overlap with those of interleukin 1 in that it acts as a growth factor, stimulant of hepatic acute phase protein synthesis, B-cell differentiation and antibody secretion and also induces fever. While measurements of cytokines or their receptor complexes are shedding light on the mechanism of the inflammatory processes in shock, the clinical role of these measurements has yet to be defined.

EICOSANOIDS

Phospholipase A2 acts on cell membrane phospholipid to form eicosasoids (this term is derived from eicosatetraenoic acid, the systematic name for arachadonic acid). The products of this reaction fall into four main classes of compound: prostaglandins, prostacyclins, thromboxanes and leucotrienes. Eicosanoid production is a property of all cells in the body with the exception of red blood cells. Eicosanoids are released from cells in response to tissue injury, hypoxia, ischaemia, endotoxin, antigen-antibody complexes, bacterial peptides, oxygen-derived free radicals and hormones

Despite the therapeutic effects of specific eicosasnoid-blocking agents in, for example, critical illness such as burns, hypovolaemic shock or adult respiratory distress syndrome, many properties of individual eicosanoids appear to be mutually antagonistic, and no clear clinical role has yet emerged either for their measurement or the use of specific blocking agents.

ENDOCRINOLOGICAL INTERVENTION IN SHOCK

Although endocrine activity undergoes profound changes in shock, the use of exogenous hormone agonists or their specific antagonists has not found an established place in the treatment of the critically ill. Treatment of the apparent abnormalities of thyroid function in the critically ill does not improve survival and may be detrimental in patients with bacterial sepsis. Although a reduced cortisol response in shock is a poor prognostic sign, steroid administration in patients with sepsis or ARDS has been of no clinical benefit. Specific antagonists to endotoxin or TNF have also found very limited application in bacterial sepsis. The use of adrenergic agonists in the treatment of shock has already been discussed.

FURTHER READING

Tobin MJ.Essentials of Critical Care Medicine. New York, Churchill Livingstone, 1989.

THE LUNGS

Ashbaugh DG, Bigelow DB, Petty TL, Levine BE. Acute respiratory distress in adults. Lancet 1967 : 319-323.

Fein AM, Goldberg SK, Lippmann ML, Fischer R, Morgan L. Adult respiratory distress syndrome. Br J Anaesthesia 1982: **54**; 723-736.

Lung permeability and other pathophysiological lung problems in shock. Frostell CG. Acta Anesthesiol Scand 1993; **37** supp 98: 11-13.

THE KIDNEYS

Gamelli RL, Silver GM. Acute renal failure. In Deitch E (ed). Multiple Organ Failure. Thieme Medical Publshers Inc New York 1990:216-240.

Sweney P. Haemofiltration and haemodiafiltration - theoretical and practical aspects. Current anaesthesia and critical care. 1991;**2**:37-43.

THE LIVER

Bernau J, Benhamou J-P. Fulminant and sub-fulminant liver failure. In: McIntyre N, Benhamou J-P, Bircher J, Rizzetto M, Rhodes J, (eds). Oxford Textbook of Clinical Hepatology. Oxford: Oxford University Press, 1991:923-942.

Collins P, McIntyre N. The liver in cardiovascular and pulmonary disease. *ibid:*1160-1170.

Sherlock S, Dooley J. Diseases of the Liver and Biliary System (9th edition). Oxford, Blackwell Scientific Publications, 1992.

Williams R, Wendon J. Management of liver failure. In: Blumgart LH (eds). Surgery of the Liver and Biliary Tree (2nd edition). Edinburgh, Churchill Livingstone, 1994: 1621-1628.

THE GUT

MacNaughton P,Evans TW, Adult Respiratory Distress Syndrome, Medicine International 1991: **91**; 3776-3780.

Fiddian-Green RG. Splanchnic ischaemia and multiple organ failure in the critically ill. Annals of the Royal College of Surgeons 1988: **70**; 128-134.

Saadia R, Schein M, MacFarland C, Boffard KD. Gut barrier function and the surgeon. Br J Surgery 1990: **77**; 487-492.

Guitierrez G,Bismar H, Dantzker DR, Silva N. Comparison of gastric intramucosal pH with measures of oxygen transport and consumption in critically ill patients. Critical Care Medicine 1992: **20** ; 451-457.

Deitch EA. Gut failure: Its role in multiple organ failure syndrome. In: Deitch EA ed. Multiple organ failure. Theime Medical Publishers Inc New York 1990: 40-59.

THE ENDOCRINE AND NERVOUS SYSTEMS

Hawker F. Endocrine changes in the critically ill. British Journal of Hospital Medicine April 1988; **39**: 278-296.

Hoffman BB, Lefkowitz RJ. Catecholamines and sympathomimetic drugs. In: Gilmann AG, Rall T, Nies A, Taylor P eds. The pharmacological basis of therapeutics. Pergamon Press New York 1990: 187-220.

Chapter 4

Case Histories

CASE 1 — SEVERE PANCREATITIS

A 35 year old man was admitted via casualty with a two day history of abdominal pain. He was pale, sweating with shallow respiration and had a tender abdomen with guarding.

Plasma	urea	6.6 mmol/L
	creatinine	126 μmol/L
	sodium	139 mmol/L
	potassium	4.5 mmol/L
	calcium	2.34 mmol/L
	aspartate transaminase	786 IU/L
	bilirubin	85 μmol/L
	albumin	45 g/L
	amylase	9100 IU/L (ref range <220)
	C-reactive protein	27 mg/L (ref range <10 mg)
Blood	glucose	8.4 mmol/L
	white cell count	14.6×10^9 /L (ref range 4.8-10.8)

Based on the clinical and laboratory findings, a diagnosis of acute pancreatitis was made. He was treated with analgesics, antibiotics, i.v. colloids and dextrose saline and nasogastric aspiration.

Comment

On admission the high white cell count and serum amylase activity confirmed the clinical diagnosis of acute pancreatitis. The elevated serum bilirubin concentration and aspartate aminotransferase activity probably reflected extrahepatic obstruction due to gall stones.

The following day he was slightly better. Ultrasound scan showed gall stones and a dilated common bile duct. However, by the evening the patient had becomed cyanosed, with tachypnoea requiring oxygen by mask. The patient was transferred to ITU, intubated and ventilated.

Plasma	urea	6.4 mmol/L
	creatinine	107 µmol/L
	sodium	144 mmol/L
	potassium	4.2 mmol/L
	calcium	1.92 mmol/L
	aspartate transaminase	439 IU/L
	bilirubin	36 µmol/L
	albumin	38 g/L
	amylase	3630 IU/L
	C-reactive protein	76 mg/L
Blood	glucose	11.1 mmol/L
	white cell count	14.6×10^9 /L
	$[H^+]$	45 nmol/L (pH 7.35)
	$PaCO_2$	6.1 kPa (46 mm Hg)
	PaO_2	3.7 kPa (28 mm Hg)

Hypocalcaemia frequently accompanies severe pancreatitis. The mechanism is unclear, in this case hypoalbuminaemia is unlikely to be the cause. The raised plasma glucose concentration is probably due to the glucogenic effect of stress hormones.

A chest X-ray suggested early adult respiratory syndrome (ARDS). The central venous pressure was low and 3 L of fluids were given as crystalloids and fresh frozen plasma.

Plasma	urea	7.4 mmol/L
	creatinine	127 umol/L
	sodium	141 mmol/L
	potassium	4.3 mmol/L
	calcium	1.51 mmol/L
	aspartate transaminase	163 IU/L
	bilirubin	37 µmol/L
	albumin	33g/L
	amylase	1470 IU/L
	C-reactive protein	319 mg/L

Blood	$[H^+]$	8 nmol/L (pH 7.55)
	$PaCO_2$	5.1 kPa (38 mm Hg)
	PaO_2	9.8 kPa (74 mm Hg)
Urine	volume	2100 ml/24hrs
	sodium	20 mmol/24hrs
	potassium	134 mmol/24hrs
	osmolality	750 mmol/kg

Comment

The mild elevations of plasma urea and creatinine concentrations are due to the hypovolaemic state of the patient caused by the loss of fluid and protein into the extravascular space and possibly the peritoneal cavity. Note the fall in plasma albumin of 7 g/L. The rapid rise in C-reactive protein indicates the severity of the inflammatory process. The mild non-respiratory alkalosis is probably due to loss of gastric secretions from nasogastric aspiration. The urinary results indicate appropriate retention of sodium and water.

The patient had deteriorated further by day 3 and required high positive end expiratory pressures for adequate oxygenation. Chest x-ray showed features of ARDS, and repeat ultrasound scan failed to show any significant fluid collection. It was felt the patient was too ill to undergo exploratory surgery. Despite intravenous fluid administration the patient was hypotensive with a falling urine output and low cardiac index. Low dose dopamine was given to maintain urine flow and dobutamine given to improve cardiac output. Since enteral feed was not absorbed, TPN was started.

Comment

The pyrexia (temperature was 40.0°C) and leukocytosis (white cell count 45.4×10^9/L) with very high plasma C-reactive protein concentrations (266 mg/L) in the apparent absence of a pathogenic organism is a common finding in the critically ill. Explanatory theories include organism supression by antibiotics, or the release of endotoxin into the circulation from the gut due to increased intestinal permeability. The development of oedema resulting from increased microvascular leakage of protein and fluid makes the lungs 'stiff', requiring high ventilation pressures.

On day 4 the patient developed a pneumothorax which required insertion of a chest drain. Urine output had fallen despite inotropes, low dose dopamine and positive fluid balance, and fluid input was reduced to avoid fluid overload. The patient was becoming oedematous.

Plasma	urea	6.3 mmol/L
	creatinine	110 umol/L
	sodium	153 mmol/L
	potassium	4.2 mmol/L
	calcium	1.92 mmol/L
	aspartate transaminase	95 IU/L
	bilirubin	11 μmol/L
	albumin	28 g/L
	amylase	1354 IU/L
	C-reactive protein	323 mg/L
Blood	glucose	13.8 mmol/L
	$[H^+]$	50 nmol/L (pH 7.30)
	$P\text{aCO}_2$	6.0 kPa (45 mm Hg)
	$P\text{aO}_2$	9.8 kPa (74 mm Hg)
Urine	Volume	1100 ml/24hrs
	sodium	17 mmol/24 hrs
	potassium	107 mmol/24 hrs
	osmolality	600 mmol/kg

Comment

The fall in urine output with high urine osmolality suggests renal underperfusion, hence the use of low dose dopamine (a β-2 agonist causing renal vasodilatation) to improve renal blood flow. Critically ill patients often become oedematous due to increased vascular permeability and because of heart failure, with leakage of large volumes of protein-containing fluid into the interstitial space. Thus a patient can be grossly fluid overloaded whilst being 'hypovolaemic' with respect to the vascular space with consequent under perfusion of vital organs.

Lung function was worse by day 5, and maintenance of cardiac output required increasingly large doses of inotropes. Urine output continued to fall despite administration of frusemide. A low sodium TPN regime was established with additional calcium and phosphate.

Plasma	urea	9.5 mmol/L
	creatinine	129 µmol/L
	sodium	158 mmol/L
	potassium	4.2 mmol/L
	C-reactive protein	328 mg/L
	phosphate	0.17 mmol/L
Blood	$[H^+]$	56 nmol/L (pH 7.25)
	$PaCO_2$	6.3 kPa (47 mmHg)
	PaO_2	8.5 kPa (64 mm Hg)
Urine	Volume	1500 ml/24hrs
	sodium	71 mmol/24 hrs
	potassium	92 mmol/24 hrs
	osmolality	400 mmol/kg

Comment

The hypernatraemia is probably due to sodium conservation due to the renal response to under perfusion and high sodium intake from the TPN regime and antibiotics. The steadily falling albumin is due in part to the continued leak of protein into the interstitial space. Hypophosphataemia is not unusual in the critically ill, partly because of the use of insulin to promote glucose uptake by the cells also permits cellular phosphate uptake, and because of increased urinary phosphate losses. Despite the high plasma osmolality, the urine osmolality of only 400 mmol/kg suggests some degree of renal unresponsiveness to vasopressin.

On day 6 the patient's cardiac output fell disasterously, urine output fell to almost zero and hypoxaemia worsened despite high inspired oxygen fraction of 1.0. The patient died in the early afternoon.

Plasma	urea	13.3 mmol/L
	creatinine	218 μmol/L
	sodium	145 mmol/L
	potassium	5.4 mmol/L
	glucose	19.3 mmol/L

Comment

The falling cardiac output produces a cycle of reduced perfusion and worsening oedema. Thus for the vascular bed of all organs there is an increasing arterial-venous shunt with less and less tissue perfusion. In the lungs, oxygenation of blood becomes inadequate, and this together with the failure of tissue perfusion prevents oxygen delivery. The rising plasma urea and creatinine concentrations indicate intrinsic renal failure, the hyperglycaemia is probably due to failure of intracellular glucose utilisation.

Approximately 80% of patients with acute pancreatitis make an uncomplicated recovery with conservative management alone. The remaining 20% develop complications such as formation of pseudocysts, chronic pancreatitis and 'sepsis syndrome' with multiple organ failure. The mortality of this latter group is about 50%. The most frequent causes of acute pancreatitis are gall stones, alcohol and to a lesser extent, viral infections.

CASE 2 — DEHYDRATION IN A 23 MONTH OLD CHILD WITH 40% SCALDS.

A 10 kg 23 month old girl was admitted with 40% scalds. The patient was resuscitated with colloids and crystalloids. The patient was fed enterally via a nasogastric tube.

By day 3 urine output had fallen and by day 5 the patient had become hypotensive, pyrexial, had developed diarrhoea, tachycardia and a rash. She failed to absorb feed from a nasogastric tube. Toxic shock syndrome was suspected and the patient was transferred to the ITU.

A central venous line was inserted which showed low filling pressures , suggesting hypovolaemia. The patient was treated with i.v. crystalloids, colloids, potassium and antibiotics.

The patient's condition improved, enteral feeding was restarted and the falling plasma C-reactive protein concentration indicated effective treatment of sepsis. However by day 9, the patient developed hyponatraemia. The patient's fluid intake was reviewed and she was found to have developed a positive fluid balance of 1 L over the preceeding 3 days. Her fluid intake was reduced on the morning of day 10, and by day 11 her hyponatraemia had started to resolve.

Comment

Patients with major burns lose large volumes of fluid and electrolytes both through the burn injury and into the extravascular space as part of the systemic response to injury. By day 3, despite resucitation, the patient became dehydrated. Plasma urea and creatinine concentrations for a child of her size were increased (body surface area 0.46 square metres), and the urine showed sodium conservation relative to potassium. The mild hyponatraemia and low serum osmolality probably reflect sodium depletion. Falling urine output with hyponatraemia and low plasma osmolality might have led to a diagnosis of inappropriate diuresis. However the low urinary sodium and increase in plasma urea and creatinine rule out this possibility.

Following transfer to the ITU and rehydration, urine volumes and sodium excretion increased to supra normal levels with low plasma and urine osmolalities, and a fall in plasma sodium concentration. Volume expansion by administration of large volumes of fluid produces both a dilutional hyponatraemia and inhibits renin and aldosterone secretion, allowing large quantities of sodium to be lost in the urine. This state was corrected by reduction of fluid administration to produce negative fluid balance and by providing an adequate sodium intake.

The laboratory data for Case 2 is shown overleaf

Day	1	2	3	4	5	6	7	8	9	10	11
SERUM											
Na mmol/L	137	131	130	136	145	141	138	136	130	131	135
K mmol/L	3.7	NA	3.2	2.9	3.1	5.0	4.7	4.2	3.5	4.3	4.0
Urea mmol/L	8.1	5.7	6.1	8.8	4.7	2.7	3.3	2.4	2.2	2.4	2.9
Creatinine μmol/L	56		88		47	51	22	25	29	35	41
Albumin g/L					37		35	34	31	32	33
Osmolality mmol/kg			271	279	299					271	279
C-reactive protein mg/L					150	96	62	45	57	50	54
URINE											
Volume mL/24h	140*	244	RU	RU	RU	368	107	998	833	850	300
Na mmol/24hr**	28	24	13	5	2	74	223	184	26	175	36
K mmol/24hr**	10	19	77	25	18	26	88	53	11	40	15
Osmolality mmol/kg					678	108	110	153	170	200	500
Creatinine clearance mL/min							35		30		24

* 8 hour collection,
** RU=random urine mmol/L
NA=not available

CASE 3 — RESPIRATORY FAILURE

On admission, a previously fit 75 year old male presented with a 10 day history of myalgia, pyrexia and dry cough, temperature of 38.5 °C, sodium 123 mmol/L, WBC 17.1×10^9/L and pulse oximeter saturation (SpO_2) 75% on room air, SpO_2 88% with FiO_2 0.35 and SpO_2 91% on FiO_2 0.4. A diagnosis of Legionella chest infection was made and treatment with intravenous erythromycin and oxygen started.

Day 3
Patient deteriorated with a clinical diagnosis of fluid overload and was treated with diuretics (i.v. frusemide).

Day 5
Referred for Intensive Care because of a further deterioration in respiratory function. Chest X-ray showed bilateral pulmonary infiltrates. Arterial blood gases when breathing spontaneously with an FiO_2 of 0.6:

$[H^+]$	34.5 nmol/L (pH 7.46)
$PaCO_2$	4.9 kPa (37 mm Hg)
PaO_2	3.9 kPa (29 mm Hg)
SaO_2	60%

The patient was now severely hypoxic and in imminent danger of a cardiac arrest due to hypoxia. Therefore the trachea was intubated and mechanical ventilation started with FiO_2 of 1.0, tidal volume of 800 mL at a rate of 12/min and PEEP titrated to 15 cms H_2O to reach a pulse oximeter reading of 90%. Arterial blood gases showed:

$[H^+]$	47.7 nmol/L (pH 7.32)
$PaCO_2$	6.6 kPa (50 mm Hg)
PaO_2	8.7 kPa (65 mm Hg)
SaO_2	89%
Hb	8.2 g/dL
CaO_2	10.4 mL/L

In view of the barely adequate oxygenation despite an FiO_2 of 1.0 and high levels of PEEP, a pulmonary artery catheter was inserted to differentiate cardiogenic from non-cardiogenic pulmonary oedema. The wedge pressure of only 12 mmHg indicated non-cardiogenic pulmonary oedema.

Cardiac index	3.0 L/min/M²
PvO_2	5.0 kPa (38 mm Hg)
CvO_2	6.8 mL/L
DO_2	380 mL/min/M²
VO_2	108 mL/min/M²

This showed oxygen delivery was low due to both a low Hb and a low cardiac index. Three units of blood were given rapidly and the inotropes dobutamine and noradrenaline were started to increase the cardiac output and maintain blood pressure.

After stabilisation, repeat measurements 3 hours later while ventilated with an FiO_2 0.6, tidal volume of 800 ml/L, rate of 12/min and PEEP 15 cms:

Wedge pressure	16 mmHg
Cardiac Index	4.6 L/min/M²
$[H^+]$	38.6 nmol/L (pH 7.44)
$PaCO_2$	5.2 kPa (39 mm Hg)
PaO_2	11.5 kPa (86 mm Hg)
SaO_2	97%
Hb	12.1 g/dL
CaO_2	16.4 mL/L
SvO_2	75%
CvO_2	12.7 mL/L
DO_2	754 mL/L/M²
VO_2	170 mL/L/M²

Day 5 The patient required haemofiltration for control of renal failure and fluid balance.

On day 9 the patient died from multiple organ failure (respiratory, cardiovascular, renal, and gastro-intestinal) due to a Legionella chest infection.

Comment

This case illustrates some of the principles of manipulation of both respiratory and cardiovascular systems to ensure adequate oxygenation. Unfortunately in this case, despite achieving systemic oxygenation, the underlying pathological processes had progressed too far for recovery.

CASE 4 — ACUTE LIVER FAILURE

A 40 year old woman was admitted via casualty suffering from acute central abdominal pain, nausea and vomiting for the last 7 days. She was a heavy smoker and had been a heavy drinker. She had suffered a recent chest infection for which she had taken antibiotics. The patient was known to have taken an overdose of diazepam two years ago and was currently taking tricyclic antidepressants. On examination she was apyrexial, with epigastric tenderness and scattered wheezes in her chest. Haemoglobin, white cell and platelet count were normal as were plasma sodium, potassium, urea, creatinine and serum amylase. Abdominal ultrasound was unhelpful. The next day the pain had settled but she continued to suffer right upper quadrant abdominal tenderness. That evening the patient became very unwell with tachycardia and hypotension (BP 70/50 mmHg):

Plasma	urea	15.9 mmol/L (4.6 on admission)
	creatinine	400 µmol/L (112 on admission)
	sodium	133 mmol/L
	potassium	5.9 mmol/L
	aspartate transaminase	607 IU/L
	bilirubin	5 µmol/L
	alkaline phosphatase	198 IU/L (ref range 70-350)
	albumin	33 g/L
	amylase	106 IU/L (ref range <220)
	paracetamol	undetectable
Blood	glucose	0.6 mmol/L
	$[H^+]$	57 nmol/L (pH 7.25)
	$PaCO_2$	2.7 kPa (20 mm Hg)
	PaO_2	13.8 kPa (104 mm Hg)

	platelets	109 x 10^9/L (227 on admission)
	INR*	4.1 (ref range 0.8-1.2)
Urine	sodium	3 mmol/L
	potassium	40 mmol/L
	urea	25 mmol/L

The patient was given intravenous dextrose and transferred to the ITU, where a central venous line was inserted which revealed low filling pressures. Four units of fresh frozen plasma were given. The patient continued to breath spontaneously with oxygen given by mask. The patient was very drowsy but rousable.

Comment

The hypotension, non respiratory acidosis and hypoglycaemia were considered to be due to septicaemia possible from an intra abdominal site. The fall in platelets and a prolonged clotting time (INR) was thought to be due to development of disseminated intravascular coagulation (DIC). The rapid deterioration in renal function was attributed to renal hypoperfusion (pre renal failure) which is supported by the low urinary sodium excretion.

Low dose dopamine was given to promote urine flow and dobutamine and adrenaline were required to maintain cardiac output and peripheral circulation, and further fresh frozen plasma and platelets were given to treat the DIC. The patient was treated with broad spectrum antibiotics although no significant organism was found from swabs or blood culture. Examination revealed no evidence of an intra abdominal or vaginal cause for the patient's apparent sepsis.

Results later that day were as follows:

Plasma	urea	5.8 mmol/L
	creatinine	395 µmol/L
	sodium	142 mmol/L
	potassium	4.6 mmol/L
	aspartate transaminase	12,060 IU/L
	bilirubin	42 µmol/L

*(International Normalised Ratio)

	alkaline phosphatase	218 IU/L
	albumin	27 g/L
	C-reactive protein	69 mg/L (ref range <10)
Blood	glucose	10.3 mmol/L
	haemoglobin	12.3 g/dL
	white cell count	11.8×10^9/L

At this point a diagnosis of fulminant liver failure was made and the patient was transferred to the liver unit.

Comment

The extremely rapid rise in aspartate aminotransferase indicates severe hepatocellular breakdown, and the absence of a leucocytosis and very high C-reactive protein (C-RP) is inconsistent with septicaemia (although theoretically hepatic synthesis of C-RP may be impaired in very severe liver disease). The persistent elevation of plasma creatinine concentration despite restoration of the circulation by administration of colloids and crystalloids indicates that intrinsic renal impairment is now present. Note the disproportionately low plasma urea concentration, which is due to the failure of hepatic urea synthesis. The patient's drowsy state is typical of hepatic encephalopathy. The patient's hypoglycaemia may be attributed to the absence of hepatic glycogen stores and the failure of hepatic gluconeogensis, and the latter may have also caused a lactic acidosis.

On the liver unit, urine output was poor (5-10 mL per hour) and the patient's cardiovascular system was unstable, requiring continued administration of inotropes. Fresh frozen plasma and platelets were required to maintain normal clotting function, and sodium bicarbonate was given to correct the non-respiratory acidosis. Since the patient's renal function did not improve, continuous arteriovenous haemodiafiltration (CAVHD) was started. Lactulose was given to discourage the proliferation of ammonia-producing intestinal bacteria and reduce the risk of hepatic encephalopathy. After 2 days on the liver unit, results were as follows

Plasma	urea	17.7 mmol/L
	creatinine	317 μmol/L
	sodium	138 mmol/L
	potassium	4.2 mmol/L
	aspartate transaminase	208 IU/L
	bilirubin	191 μmol/L
	alkaline phosphatase	335 IU/L
	albumin	26 g/L

Comment

The fall in aspartate aminotransferase activity does not necessarily reflect improvement in fulminant liver failure, but may indicate the absence of intact hepatic parenchymal cells. The rise in bilirubin shows increasing cholestasis. The stabilisation of plasma creatinine concentration is due to the CAVHD.

During the subsequent days plasma bilirubin steadily fell as did aspartate transaminase. By day 21 (11 days on the liver unit) results were as follows:

Plasma	urea	32.9 mmol/L
	creatinine	299 μmol/L
	sodium	142 mmol/L
	potassium	3.9 mmol/L
	aspartate transaminase	109 IU/L
	bilirubin	110 μmol/L
	alkaline phosphatase	676 IU/L
	albumin	26 g/L

Renal function improved and CAVHD was stopped three days later.

Comment

The rise in alkaline phosphatase at a time when bilirubin was falling may represent improving hepatic synthetic function in response to continued cholestasis.

The patient continued to improve and by day 41 the results were as follows:

Plasma	urea	4.9 mmol/L
	creatinine	125 μmol/L
	sodium	139 mmol/L
	potassium	4.0 mmol/L
	aspartate transaminase	67 IU/L
	bilirubin	39 μmol/L
	alkaline phosphatase	351 IU/L
	albumin	35 g/L

Comment

The cause of this patient's acute liver failure was never identified. Hepatitis serology was negative. The patient denied taking paracetamol during her chest infection, but confirmed her high alcohol intake and dependency on tricyclic antidepressants.

CASE 5 — SEPTICAEMIA

A 41-year old man was admitted to hospital and immediately transferred to the Intensive Care Unit. He was a methadone addict, and was known to have alcoholic liver disease and oesophageal varices. The recent history was of one week's cough with brown sputum, and two days of shortness of breath.

On examination, he was drowsy, tachypnoeic (respiratory rate 40/min), tachycardic (pulse 140/min), pyrexial (39.2°C) and peripherally cyanosed. In the chest, there were widespread coarse crepitations with diminished air entry, more so on the right. He had hepatomegaly and gynaecomastia.

Chest X-Ray showed opcification of the whole of the right lung, consistent with the clinical diagnosis of aspiration pneumonia.

Arterial blood gases in the emergency room are shown in the table (A); he was given intravenous bicarbonate. After admission to the ITU, breathing 40% oxygen, blood gases were as shown (B); inspired oxygen was increased to 60% (C).

	(A)	(B)	(C)	
$[H^+]$	160	65	58	nmol/L
pH	6.79	7.19	7.24	
PaO_2	6.1	10.1	6.2	kPa
$PaCO_2$	5.9	6.6	5.3	kPa
SaO_2	41.2		74.6	%

Comment:

The data on admission indicate severe hypoxaemia, with a disproportionately low saturation due to the severe metabolic acidosis (thought to have been a direct consequence of the hypoxaemia) and consequent right shift in the oxyhaemoglobin dissociation curve. Partial correction of the acidosis increased the saturation even though the PaO_2 did not change.

In view of the continued hypoxia, he was paralyzed and ventilated. Following intubation, systolic blood pressure fell to 60 mmHg; 300 mL of plasma expander were infused and blood pressure increased to 100 mmHg.

Despite adequate central venous pressures, systolic blood pressure fell to between 70 and 90 mmHg and was resistant to further infusion of plasma expander. An infusion of noradrenaline was commenced. Urine output dropped to zero. A urinary catheter was placed and an infusion of dopamine at a 'renal dose' (3 µg/kg/min) was commenced.

Haemoglobin was 11.1 g/dL, white blood cell count 1.9×10^9/L, platelets 17×10^9/L; the prothrombin time was twice normal. Disseminated intravascular coagulation was suspected. At this stage, medication included broad spectrum antibiotics, ranitidine, vitamin K, folic acid and Parenterovite. Intravenous fluids were 5% dextrose and plasma expander to match output.

He remained anuric. There was little change over the next 12 hours but his haemoglobin fell to 9 g/dL although there was no overt bleeding.

Systematic review at this stage:

CVS	Pulse 124 BP 120/60 Adequate filling pressures On dopamine and noradrenaline

Respiratory	Sedated and ventilated; IPPV with 5 cm H_2O PEEP Continued hypoxia (PaO_2 10.7 kPa on FiO_2 100%)
Liver	Prolonged prothrombin time (INR 1.6) despite fresh frozen plasma Albumin 21 g/L, bilirubin 105 µmol/L, AST 195 IU/L, ALP 421 IU/L
Renal	Anuric Urea 18.7 mmol/L, creatinine 203 µmol/L
General	Septic, pyrexial (T=38-39°C); on multiple antibiotics Falling haemoglobin (due to haemodilution?).

It was decided to continue full antibiotic cover, start renal replacement treatment and institute nutritional support with parenteral feeding.

Comment

He had multisystem (cardiovascular, respiratory and renal) failure in addition to chronic liver disease and probable systemic sepsis. The low albumin may have been due to his liver disease but could also have been related to increased capillary permeability and increased volume of distribution. Although enteral feeding was contemplated, he was known to have oesophageal varices and the risk of these being damaged and bleeding due to the passage of a nasogasric tube was considered to be too high so that he was fed parenterally, 'space' being made for the feed (and for drugs) by removal of fluid by renal replacement (continuous arteriovenous haemofiltration).

Over the next 48 hours, his condition deteriorated. He continued to require an FiO_2 of 100% and noradrenaline but his maximum PaO_2 was 9 kPa and his blood pressure averaged 100/40. He remained anuric. The urinary catheter was removed because of the danger of infection. He was given transfusions of platelets, red cells and albumin.

His blood pressure fell and could not be maintained despite an increase in the dose of noradrenaline; blood was seen in the nasopharynx but before he could be gastroscoped, he sustained a cardiac arrest and died.

CASE 6 —MULTIPLE ORGAN FAILURE

A 70-year old man was admitted to hospital one evening with a 14h history of colicky abdominal pain. He had vomited three times, he had a normal bowel motion that morning.

He was a non-insulin dependent diabetic, treated with metformin, and was on digoxin and Navidrex-K for cardiac failure. Past medical history was otherwise unremarkable.

On examination, he was in atrial fibrillation, but there were no signs of cardiac failure. There was a tense, irreducible, hot swelling in the right groin. A diagnosis of strangulated right inguinal hernia was made and he was taken to theatre. The diagnosis was confirmed at operation; the incarcerated bowel was considered viable and the hernia was repaired uneventfully.

Next morning, he developed açute left ventricular failure, his blood pressure falling to 80/40 mmHg. He was treated with diuretics, diamorphine, intramuscular digoxin and aminophylline. A broad spectrum antibiotic was started.

At midday, he became shocked, with systolic blood pressure 90 mmHg and diastolic unrecordable. He was pyrexial (39.5°C) and had some abdominal guarding and rebound. He was tachypnoeic (respiratory rate 40/min).

Plasma	urea	15.5 mmolL	(9.5 on admission)
	creatinine	191 µmolL	(86 on admission)
	sodium	140 mmol/L	
	potassium	5.1 mmolL	
Blood	glucose	21.1 mmolL	
	$[H^+]$	38 nmol/L (pH 7.42)	
	$PaCO_2$	2.9 kPa (22 mmHg)	
	PaO_2	8.7 kPa (65 mmHg)	
	derived $[HCO_3^-]$	13 mmol/L	

A clinical diagnosis of septicaemia was made - secondary either to bladder catheterisation on admission or to possible bowel necrosis. Blood cultures were taken and further antibiotics were started. He was transferred to Intensive Care.

Comment

He was developing renal failure and had a mixed respiratory alkalosis and metabolic acidosis. The acidosis was considered to be secondary to poor peripheral perfusion and renal failure and the alkalosis to hyperventilation due to the hypoxia.

A central venous catheter was placed in order to monitor his fluid status and intravenous fluids (plasma expander and dextrose saline) were given to maintain a CVP of +15 cm H_2O. He was intubated and given an FiO_2 of 40%. A 'renal dose' of dopamine (3 μg/kg/min) was started. He was started on a continuous infusion of insulin.

Over the next nine hours, his hourly urine output fell: 55, 50, 60, 45, 60, 80, 20, 20 10 mL, despite further doses of frusemide. He became frankly acidotic, [H^+] 89 nmol/L (pH 7.19), and was given an infusion of bicarbonate. His urine output improved for a time but he remained hypotensive.

Forty hours after admission he again became oliguric. Results are shown in the table (A). He was given further bicarbonate, and calcium resonium per rectum (B).

		(A)	(B)	
Plasma	sodium	136	141	mmol/L
	potassium	6.2	6.0	mmol/L
	urea	25	26.2	mmol/L
	creatinine	423	460	μmol/L
	osmolality	322		mmol/kg
Blood	glucose	22.4	21.2	mmol/L
	[H^+]	76	24	nmol/L
	pH	7.12	7.6	
	PaO_2	7.8	5.7	kPa
	$PaCO_2$	7.4	7.3	kPa
	derived [HCO_3^-]	18	57	mmol/L
Urine	sodium	94		mmol/L
	osmolality	320		mmol/kg

Comment

He appeared to have established renal failure, with equal plasma and urine osmolalities and a high urinary sodium. The latter can be caused by diuretics in the pre-renal phase but he had not had a dose of frusemide for several hours. Note the 'overshoot' in bicarbonate caused by giving too large a dose. Two hours later, plasma bicarbonate had fallen to 22 mmol/L, due to the persisting tendency to acidosis. The secretion of counter-regulatory hormones (catecholamines, cortisol, glucagon and growth hormone) opposes the actions of insulin and many critically ill patients with non-insulin dependent diabetes require insulin for the control of glycaemia. It should be noted that metformin, a biguanide oral hypoglycaemic agent, has been implicated in the development of lactic acidosis, particularly in patients with impaired renal function, although this man's renal function appeared normal on admission.

Over the next twelve hours, he continued to be hypotensive despite treatment with inotropes. Renal replacement was commenced. He underwent a mini-laparotomy in Intensive Care but all the bowel was intact and there was no evidence of peritonitis. Fifty hours after admission, he had a cardiac arrest from which he could not be resuscitated.

Comment

This man's renal failure was a consequence of hypotension and impaired renal perfusion. The cause of the hypotension remained uncertain. He may have sustained a myocardial infarction although there was no cardiographic or biochemical evidence of this. The clinical picture is typical of septicaemia and post mortem the blood cultures were reported as growing E.coli.

This case emphasizes the complexity of multiorgan failure, and the necessity for adequate monitoring of vital functions and haematological and biochemical variables. Most of the biochemical tests that are required for patients in intensive care are standard ones. What is essential is that their results are made available rapidly, and for those which determine immediate management, for example, blood gases, this should be done (by suitably trained staff using properly maintained equipment) using instruments sited near the patient.

Note that his plasma urea concentration would have provided a poor indication of renal function in view of his liver disease and that there are many potential causes of low albumin concentrations in critically ill patients.

Nutritional support should always be provided enterally if possible but if this is contraindicated, parenteral feeding will be required. Particularly in patients with a history of chronic alcohol abuse, it is essential to provide large doses of B vitamins as prophylaxis against Wernicke's encephalopathy.

Uncontrollable bleeding is a common terminal event in patients with severe liver disease.

Chapter 5

Clinical Biochemistry Services for the Intensive Care Unit

The organisation of clinical biochemistry services for the intensive care unit can conveniently be split into those investigations required urgently, several times a day, which effect immediate patient management: those investigations which are generally required on a daily basis, and those which reflect more gradual processes and can be provided two to three times a week or less frequently.

Some investigations in the first category can only be provided by continuous *in vivo* monitoring, while others are best provided by 'near patient testing', i.e., using equipment sited in the ITU. Less urgent analyses can be provided by central laboratories, but ideally intensive care physicians and clinical biochemists should agree protocols to ensure defined and appropriate provision of analytical services.

FREQUENT INVESTIGATIONS

PARAMETERS OF OXYGENATION

The assessment of oxygen delivery was reviewed in Chapter 2. In addition to the measurement of blood oxygen tension (PO_2) direct estimation of oxyhaemoglobin and deoxyhaemoglobin by oximetry can be used to calculate the total oxygen content of blood, whilst measurements made on arterial and mixed venous blood can be used to derive pulmonary shunt data. Automatic calculation of these parameters is now available on a number of computer systems specifically designed to work in tandem with blood gas analysers and oximeters. Simultaneous oximetry also provides accurate values for total haemoglobin, carboxyhaemoglobin and methaemoglobin, which are valuable in the management of patients suffering from carbon monoxide inhalation and in certain cases of poisoning.

Oxygenation can also be assessed *in vivo* by measurement of oxygen saturation using a pulse oximeter. Pulse oximetry is based on the measurement of the change in optical absorption of light due to variations in tissue volume with each heart beat. In order optimally to measure oxyhaemoglobin and deoxyhaemoglobin, wavelengths are chosen in the red and infra red spectrum. At zero arterial haemoglobin saturation, the pulse absorption amplitude in the red spectrum is larger than that in the infra red, while at 100% oxygen saturation the infra red absorption pulse amplitude is greater than that in the red spectrum. The ratio of the red to infra red absorption amplitudes during each arterial pulsation is thus proportional to the oxygen saturation of haemoglobin. Since venous blood does not generally pulsate, it does not contribute to the change in optical absorption, and is therefore not included in the assessment of arterial haemoglobin oxygen saturation.

Errors can occur due to the presence of carboxyhaemoglobin, or when the pulse amplitude is very small such as in vasoconstricted patients. Variations can also occur between expansion and contraction of the lungs if gas exchange is poor.

Pulse oximetry is clinically useful since it provides a non-invasive, real time measure of haemoglobin saturation. It can be used to monitor the patency of the airway during general anaesthesia and is widely used for the continuous monitoring of oxygenation in mechanically ventilated patients. Mild hypoxia has been identified in ITU patients by oximetry which would have been missed by intermittent blood gas measurement. Ventilator settings can be adjusted on pulse oximeter data, reinforced by blood gas analysis. Saturations of 90% are associated with mild hypoxia, while saturations of 85% or less can indicate severe hypoxia. Oxygen delivery to the tissues can be calculated by multiplying the oxygen content of arterial blood by the cardiac output, and tissue oxygen consumption can be determined by subtracting the mixed venous oxygen content multiplied by the cardiac output from the value for oxygen delivery.

NEAR PATIENT TESTING

Modern equipment allows the majority of investigations required for immediate patient management to be undertaken on whole blood by

Table 5.1 Range of near patient investigations

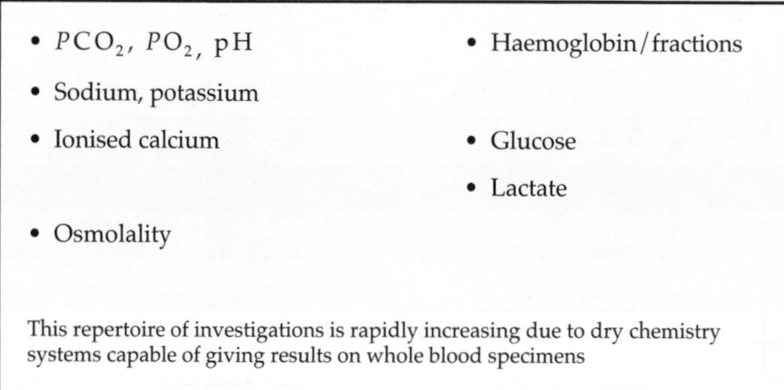

• PCO_2, PO_2, pH	• Haemoglobin/fractions
• Sodium, potassium	
• Ionised calcium	• Glucose
	• Lactate
• Osmolality	

This repertoire of investigations is rapidly increasing due to dry chemistry systems capable of giving results on whole blood specimens

non-laboratory staff in the ITU (Table 5.1). There are several advantages in carrying out these analyses near to the critically ill patient.

- Results are immediately available, helping decisions on patient management to be made quickly.
- No transport services are required, and time consuming request form completion is avoided.
- The risk of transcription errors arising from results being telephoned from the laboratory is reduced.
- The demands made on an expensive 24-hour-a-day laboratory service are also reduced.
- The provision of appropriate equipment in the ITU may remove the need for an on-site laboratory to serve the ITU, and allow centralisation of laboratory services.

However, performance of extra-laboratory testing does require that the results produced are reliable, consistent with those produced by the laboratory and not subject to artefacts due to, for example, haemolysis, incorrect sample technique, dilution with liquid anticoagulants, incorrect use of analytical equipment or the metabolic effects of undue delay in analysis. Accordingly it is essential that access to the equipment is limited to trained users only, and that the training of non-laboratory users is comprehensive and includes an understanding of the equipment's limitations. In a large hospital setting this is not always easy, but the use of a host computer linked to the instrument with a password or personal identification number can be helpful. A summary of sources of error in blood gas and electrolyte measurement is given in the Appendix 1.

A further requirement of extra-laboratory testing is reliable recording of patient results. This can also be achieved by the use of a host computer, generally located next to the instrument.

The reader is referred to Appendix 2 - 'Guidelines for Implementation of Near-Patient Testing'. Ideally the provision of ITU analytical equipment should be made in collaboration with the relevant local laboratory.

DAILY LABORATORY INVESTIGATIONS

The metabolic consequences of shock are rapid, and may require intervention to augment homeostatic mechanisms. The regular monitoring of labile parameters such as blood glucose and plasma potassium concentrations is essential on a daily or more frequent basis in the critically ill. Daily assessment of hydration and renal function is also essential and is usually done by measurement of plasma sodium, potassium, urea and creatinine and sometimes osmolality. Daily measurement of urinary volume, and of sodium, potassium and urea excretion can also provide valuable information on water and salt homeostasis (Chapter 3).

Patients in ITU are particularly prone to sepsis, and significant rises in daily serum C-reactive protein concentration are a valuable adjunct to the clinical diagnosis of bacterial sepsis, and since its half life is 36 hours, will give a useful marker of the efficacy of antibiotic treatment. The clinical and metabolic consequences of shock are closely related, and neither can be meaningfully assessed in isolation. The importance of interpreting laboratory data in the light of a thorough understanding of the relevant pathophysiology, and of all other available information cannot be overemphasised.

LESS FREQUENT MONITORING

In general, laboratory measurements which reflect more gradual changes need not be measured daily, but can be monitored on alternate days, or thrice weekly. For example, other than in exceptional circumstances (e.g., shock liver, fulminant hepatic failure) it would not be necessary to assess liver dysfunction with serum aspartate transaminase and alkaline phosphatase activities, prothrombin times and serum bilirubin concentrations more than two or three times a week. Serum phosphate concentrations should be measured daily in circumstances in which derangement can be anticipated such as the commencement of TPN, likewise magnesium should be measured in patients receiving cis-platinum or amphotericin. Assessment of micronutrient status, in particular serum zinc and copper concentrations, is not normally required in ITU patients unless they have been fed parenterally for two weeks or more, or are predisposed to deficiency, such as following a major burn injury. A suggested monitoring regime for patients on TPN is given in Table 5.2.

Table 5.2 Suggested minimum frequency of laboratory monitoring of patients receiving TPN during first 1-2 weeks of treatment

Daily	2-3 x Weekly
• blood glucose	• plasma calcium
• plasma potassium	albumin
sodium	'liver function' tests
phosphate	magnesium
urea	
creatinine	**Weekly**
• urine sodium (spot)	• plasma zinc
	copper

Therapeutic drug monitoring in the critically ill may need to be more intensive than in less seriously ill patients because of the effects of compromised organ function on pharmokinetics, and because clinical symptoms of toxicity may be masked in sedated patients. For example, optimisation of therapeutic doses of aminoglycoside antibiotics or digoxin in patients with renal impairment may require more frequent measurement of serum concentrations. Clearance of theophylline will be reduced in patients with cardiac failure, hepatic cirrhosis or pulmonary oedema. Sampling times should be adjusted in the light of predicted time taken to reach steady state blood concentrations following either dosage adjustment or commencement of therapy.

PROTOCOLS AND DATA PRESENTATION

It may be helpful to agree with ITU clinical staff protocols, for the biochemical monitoring of ITU patients, which can be used to prompt appropriate investigations; analyses can be added or deleted depending on individual patient's requirements. This may be particularly relevant following standardised major surgical procedures such as transplantation. This approach has the advantage of both avoiding unnecessarily frequent monitoring and omitting the measurement of unusual, but in particular circumstances, essential analytes.

Since many biochemical and haematological variables will be abnormal in ITU patients, the relative change hour by hour or day by day is often as, or more, important than the absolute value. Accordingly it is essential to present patient data, including pathology laboratory data, in a serial fashion such that day to day trends can be detected early. The simplest method of achieving this is a hand written flow chart with boxes conveniently laid out (Figure 5.3). More sophisticated computer-generated graphical presentations have the advantage of being less labour intensive and serial results can be easily assessed. Ideally validated laboratory data could be 'downloaded' to the ITU computer system directly, and presented on a VDU. However, there is a risk of significant results being overlooked unless the data base is regularly interrogated.

While the results of tests required for immediate patient management are frequently provided by near-patient equipment, the results of the majority of laboratory investigations on patients in ITU are not required urgently. However, it is essential that they are available for ITU ward rounds, of which there are often several a day, so that significant changes can be highlighted and appropriate action taken such as modification of TPN regimes. It is highly desirable that a member of the clinical biochemistry staff attends ITU rounds regularly in order to advise on the limitations of results (due, for example, to drug interferences, or to lipaemia or hyperbilirubinaemia), to comment on the significance of results and review the overall effectiveness of the laboratory and near patient services. Such a joint activity fosters a spirit of cooperation which can only benefit patient care, and in addition, may facilitate research in this field.

Name *John Smith* Reg No *S517806* Consultant *Jones* Ward *ITU*

Date

Serum/Plasma	Ref Values	21/3	22/3	24/3	25/3					
NA	135-145 mmol/L	138	136	134	130					
K	3.5-5.0 mmol/L	4.1	3.8	3.2	3.2					
Urea	2.5-7.5 mmol/L	5.6	5.8	5.1	4.2					
Creat	50-120 μmol/L	84	92	83	75					
Glucose	mmol/L	8.2	7.6	6.9	9.3					
Ca	2.2-2.65 mmol/L	2.10		2.05						
Bilirubin	< 22 μmol/L	7		10						
Alk Phos	79-350 iu/L	290								
Albumin	35-50 g/L	35		32						
Globulin	20-35 g/L									
AST	5-35 iu/L	46		65						
PO4	0.8-1.4 mmol/L	0.9		1.2						
Magnesium	0.7-0.95 mmol/L	0.8		0.7						
Zinc	11-18 μmol/L									
Cu	12-20 μmol/L									
CRP	< 10 mg/L	12	85	190	210					
Lactate	0.6-1.2 mmol/L									
Chloride	98-106 mmol/L									
BLOOD										
Hb	male 13.4-17 g/dL	14.1	11.6	10.9	13.2					
	fem 11.4-15 g/dL									
WCC	$4\text{-}11 \times 10^9$/L	12.1	18.5	29.1	21.3					
Platelets	$150\text{-}400 \times 10^9$/L	305		193	208					
PVC	male 0.4-0.5 L/L									
	fem 0.35-0.45 L/L									
PT	0.8-1.2	1.1		0.9						
PTTK	0.8-1.2									
FDP	< 10 μg/L									
DRUG LEVELS										
Digoxin	0.8-2.0 μg/L									
Aminoph	10-20 mg/L									
Gent	contact lab									
URINE										
Volume	mls/collection		2180	1580	2560					
Na	mmols/collection		80	20	110					
K	mmols/collection		60	75	93					
Urea	mmols/collection		575	720	590					
Creat/clear ml/min	contact lab		90	75	85					

Figure 5.3 Intensive care record sheet.

FUTHER READING

Biswas CK, Ramos JM, Agroyannis B, Kerr DNS. Blood gas analysis:the effect of air bubbles in syringe and delay in estimation. BMJ 1982;**284**:923-927

Christiansen TF. Heparin and blood sampling for pH, blood gases and direct potentiometric electrolyte analysis (AS96) Copenhagen: Radiometer A/S Denmark, 1986

Gosling, Dickson GR. Syringe injection pressure: a neglected factor in blood PO_2 determination. Ann Clin Biochem 1990;**27**:147-151

Monitoring in anaesthesia and critical care medicine. Blitt CD (ed). Churchill Livingstone, New York, 1990

Marks V. Essential considerations in the provision of near-patient testing facilities. Ann Clin Biochem 1988;**25**: 220-225

Nearer the patient. Marks V, Alberti KGMM, (eds). in: Clinical biochemistry near the patient. Churchill Livingstone, Edinburgh 1985; 168-74

Therapeutic Drug Monitoring and Clinical Biochemistry Hallworth M, Capps N, London. ACB Venture Publications 1993

Appendix 1

Sources of error in blood gas and electrolyte measurements

TYPE OF ANTICOAGULANT

EFFECT – DILUTION ERRORS, ADDITION OR SUBTRACTION OF SODIUM, POTASSIUM AND IONISED CALCIUM

Heparin is the preferred anticoagulant since EDTA (potassium ethylene diaminetetra acetic acid) or citrate will effect the pH, calcium and potassium measurements. Liquid heparin introduces a dilution error typically of about 5% for PCO_2 and about 9% for plasma sodium. This is because CO_2 equilibrates between the plasma and the red blood cells, while the sodium is largely confined to the plasma compartment. Different heparin preparations contain variable amounts of calcium, potasium and sodium which can increase measured values. Heparin can also bind ions particularly calcium, reducing the amount available for measurement.

SOLUTION

Wherever possible, purpose made syringes should be used containing the correct amount of 'balanced' dry heparin which will neither add or remove (bind) calcium, sodium or potassium ions.

BLOOD SAMPLING FROM ARTERIAL LINES

EFFECT – MISLEADING PO_2, SPECIMEN DILUTION, CLOTTED BLOOD SAMPLE

Arterial blood sampling lines are frequently used in ITU patients and are kept from clotting by introduction of heparinised saline solution. Prior to drawing a blood gas sample, it is essential that the heparinised saline is completely withdrawn from the line into a separate syringe, otherwise contamination of the the blood sample used for analysis will give misleading results. If the heparin is not completely mixed with the blood, part of the specimen may clot. This will be invisible to the user, but will block the blood gas analyser. Introduction of an air bubble, (0.1 mL in a 1.0 mL specimen) which is allowed to equilibrate with the blood at 4°C will increase the PO_2 by 15%.

SOLUTION
Ensure all heparinised saline is withdrawn from the arterial lines before sampling. Use good quality syringes which do not allow air to leak during sampling. Immediately expell any air bubbles from the syringe together with the drop of blood in the syringe tip which may not be completely heparinised then mix well by inversion.

SPECIMEN STORAGE

EFFECT –LOW PH AND PO_2, HIGH POTASSIUM AND PCO_2
Red and white blood cell metabolism continues in the syringe, increasing plasma potassium and PCO_2 and decreasing pH and PO_2. Ideally the blood gas measurements should be done immediately, and analysis should not be delayed for more than ten minutes if the specimen is kept at room temperature. If the delay before analysis is longer, metabolism can be slowed by storage of the specimen at 0-4°C in iced water for up to 30-40 minutes. Longer storage on polypropylene syringes leads to CO_2 loss through the syringe wall. Plasma potassium values rise during cold storage due to leakage from red blood cells at between 0.1-0.4 mmol/L per hour.

SOLUTION
Analyse samples immediately whenever possible.

RED CELL SEDIMENTATION

EFFECT – INCORRECT HAEMOGLOBIN, ERRONEOUS pH, PCO_2 AND PO_2
Red blood cells settle out of plasma rapidly, especially in critically ill patients. Therefore unless the specimen is mixed well a few seconds before introduction into the blood gas analyser, measurements will be

made on cell rich or cell poor blood, depending on which way up the specimen has been stored. This will profoundly effect the haemoglobin value and also lead to erroneous pH, PCO_2 and PO_2 results.

SOLUTION

Mix the blood sample well immediately before introduction into the blood gas analyser.

VIOLENT INJECTION OF SAMPLE INTO BLOOD GAS ANALYSER

EFFECT – FALSELY HIGH POTASSIUM AND PO_2 VALUES

Where the specimen is injected into the analyser, this should be done gently, because undue pressure may cause haemolysis increasing potassium results, and in some instruments may effect the PO_2 value.

SOLUTION

Inject sample gently or in the case of some instrument allow the sample to be pulled into the analyser.

Appendix 2

Guidelines for Implementation of Near-Patient Testing

These Guidelines have been prepared by a Working Party consisting of Scientific Members of the Association of Clinical Biochemists (ACB), along with Corporate Membership of the ACB and Representation from the Royal College of Pathologists.

Scientific Members of the ACB
Dr. Danielle Freedman (Chairman)
Dr. David Burnett
Dr. Jonathan Kay
Professor Iain Percy-Robb

Corporate Member of the ACB
Mr. Alex Grant

Representation from the Royal College of Pathologists.
Dr. Trevor Gray

These notes are intended to provide helpful advice for those who are considering setting up a facility for Near-Patient Testing (analyses to be performed outside the hospital laboratory).

They are intended to help you choose the correct system for your purpose and, importantly, explain the steps required to ensure that your results are accurate and consistently reliable.

The major points you will need to consider are presented as the questions you should ask before obtaining your instrument (be it by purchase, leasing or donation), followed by answers which will help you to arrive at the correct decision.

The guidelines have the support of the Royal College of Pathologists and the Royal College of General Practitioners.

1. ANALYSES AND EQUIPMENT

• *WHAT ARE YOU GOING TO MEASURE ?*

The first step in the process is deciding which tests (analytes) you are going to perform. You should agree who will be investigated and what the total number of tests will be. This will not usually be easily established where the introduction of Near Patient Testing is a new venture.

• *WHAT EQUIPMENT IS MOST SUITABLE FOR YOUR PURPOSE ?*

There are many sources of information which can help you to reach the correct decision. These include the manufacturers and local hospitals, and other clinical laboratories.

Additional advice may also possibly be obtained from professional organisations, such as the Royal College of General Practitioners, Local Medical Committees, FHSAs and University Departments of General Practice. The Medical Device Directorate (MDD) of the DoH has a programme of evaluation of new equipment, and publications arising from these evaluations can be sought directly from the Medical Device Directorate, 14 Russell Square, LONDON WC1B 5EP.

Each analytical system has limitations, and its suitability must be assessed for the specific use to which it will be put. This use will determine the required analytical performance, throughput and costs. Recipients of the equipment need to be aware of methodological limitations, such as precision, accuracy, operating range and interferences by other substances, such as drugs. It is likely that the equipment will be operated by staff who are not trained as analysts and particular importance should be attached to the robustness of the analytical system: i.e., not what its performance is in the best conditions of operation, but rather that which will be achieved in the conditions in which it will actually be used.

Near patient testing often takes place in an environment - such as a GP clinic - where results are also being obtained from a hospital laboratory. It is important that the results from the near patient testing sites and from hospital laboratories should be comparable. Unless this is the case, interpretation will be problematic and confusion may occur if discrepant results are obtained. This may affect not only the choice of equipment, but also decisions such as the units of measurement in which the results are expressed. Early discussion with the local clinical laboratory is the best way of avoiding such problems.

• *What are the likely costs ?*

The immediate cost of Near Patient Testing is determined by two main factors; the cost of the equipment and 'consumables'. The latter depends on the system chosen and may include reagents required for tests, lancets, syringes, quality control material and enrolment in supporting Quality Assurances Schemes, etc. Other overheads such as staff costs should also be included in the equation should you wish to estimate the total cost of your new test facility.

2. MAINTAINING THE EQUIPMENT

• *HOW WILL YOU LOOK AFTER THE EQUIPMENT ?*

Once the equipment is in place it will need routine maintenance. Manufacturers' instructions should be sufficient to help you achieve satisfactory maintenance and, in the event of difficulties, their Customer Services Department should provide assistance. For each item of equipment it is necessary to record its serial number, service history and a log of problems encountered in its use.

• *WHAT WILL YOU DO WHEN THE EQUIPMENT DOES NOT WORK ?*

All equipment needs planned equipment maintenance and occasional repair. The Conditions of Warranty from the supplier should be discussed with the manufacturer, and the suitability of the Service Contract should be considered. The local hospital laboratory may be able to offer service and repair. The responsibility for these should be allocated before the problems occur. It may be necessary to have a back-up procedure which may involve moving the analyses to a different item of equipment on the same site or elsewhere, such as the local hospital laboratory. This needs to be planned and agreed.

3. HEALTH AND SAFETY

• *WILL YOU BE ABLE TO INITIATE AND MAINTAIN THE REQUIRED HEALTH & SAFETY PROCEDURES ?*

All procedures involving patients and biological tests require strict adherence to professionally acceptable health & safety standards.

The safety of the patient must always be assured. This entails hygienic methods of obtaining samples of blood and performing tests. Some patients may feel faint when blood is being taken. Therefore either a chair or a couch should be provided. Staff should be trained in the appropriate First Aid procedures.

Care must be taken to ensure that the biological hazards which can arise from tests using human blood or body fluids do not put operating staff or others at risk. This requires the formulation of Safety Procedures covering operational methods, the disposal of 'sharps' and body fluids, and the routine decontamination of equipment and working surfaces. If required, specialist microbiological advice will be available from your local hospital laboratory or the Public Health Laboratory Service on these matters. Advice on potential electrical or chemical hazards, including COSHH (Control of Substances Hazardous to Health) procedures should be followed and can be obtained from either the manufacturer or the local hospital laboratory.

It is possible that the sites intended for specimen collection and analyses may not have been specifically designed for this purpose. Particular aspects - in addition to those previously mentioned - which need to be considered are physical security, confidentiality of reports and the legal requirements of the Data Protection Act. These considerations are particularly important when the site is also going to be used for other purposes.

4. PERSONNEL REQUIREMENTS

• *WHAT PARTICULAR SKILLS WILL THEY NEED ?*

The skills which are needed by the staff include patient preparation, specimen collection, chemical analysis and recording and interpretation of results. It will be necessary to review aspects of Health & Safety and the maintenance of equipment. These tasks may be carried out by one person or distributed between several. Specimen collection will most commonly be by finger-prick or venepuncture. The member of staff who collects the specimen needs to be trained in the appropriate response to adverse reaction, such as faints, and possibly in First Aid.

• *HOW WILL THE STAFF BE TRAINED ?*

It is beyond dispute that well trained staff help to ensure high quality test results. All manufacturers should be able to assist in providing comprehensive training to cover operational, interpretative and follow-up activities which will help you achieve the desired quality. This process should cover in-service training of existing staff, the induction of new staff and routine refresher training across all involved personnel. In all cases training should be tailored to the background and experience of the person concerned. The individual responsible for the training should be clearly identified. They may be an existing member of staff, the manufacturer or an outside body such as the local hospital laboratory. It is good practice to record all training procedures and conclusions as these could be used in determining staff responsibilities in Near-Patient Testing.

5. QUALITY ASSURANCE

• *CAN YOU TRUST YOUR REPORTS ?*

One of the most important aspects of quality assurance is that equipment is clean, well maintained and operated, and results recorded according to a standard procedure. Confidence that results from hospital based clinical laboratories are reliable comes from such procedures.

Although these are well understood and taken very seriously in laboratories, they have sometimes been omitted when analyses are introduced elsewhere.

There are two components of analytical Quality Assurance: *Internal Quality Control and External Quality Assessment.*

Internal Quality Control is a means of checking that results are reliable before they are issued. In order to do this, samples with known concentrations of the analyte are run through the usual procedure. The key features of a scheme are the frequency with which the checks will be performed, the material that will be used, the recording of the results and the rules which determine acceptable performance. It is good practice for the outcome to be reviewed by someone other than the analyst. Even with the best current schemes these procedures do not check all stages in the production of reports and their limitations should be understood.

External Quality Assessment differs in that its findings are not available until after the results have been issued. It allows confidence that the results are not varying over time, that they are similar to those obtained at other sites and, ideally, with other equipment and analytical approaches. It involves analysis of samples received from an external source. External Quality Assessment schemes may be operated by the manufacturer of the equipment or reagents, by external bodies such as the Wolfson Laboratories in Birmingham, or by the local hospital laboratory.

• *HOW WILL THE RESULTS BE RECORDED ?*

Quality Assurance also requires that recording of data is satisfactory.

It is necessary to record the following:

i. Name of patient
ii. Date and time of the analysis
iii. Results obtained
iv. Batch number of reagents being used
v. Name of operator.

For the individual tested this may involve the recording of age, sex, location and general practitioner. Additional information may include whether the individual was fasting and details of drug treatment.

It is necessary to record this information for use by other healthcare professionals and for the purposes of clinical review, workload analyses and audit. It may also be required for legal purposes at any time in the future. The permanent record must be able to support all of these functions.

It is possible that results of tests may be compared with those coming from elsewhere, such as local hospital laboratories. This makes it important to record the source of each result. Reports should include unit of measurement and may include a reference range. Reports may be stored on paper (which should be a bound volume, rather than loose sheets), a dedicated computer or a computer used for other functions, such as a GP system or an Occupational Health system. For each of these, you should decide how long the reports will be kept and who will have access to them. If reports are to be issued, the format should be agreed and each report should include its source.

6. INTERPRETATION OF RESULTS

• *Who will be responsible for the interpretation of results ?*

Near Patient Testing has two features which can increase the pressure on whoever is responsible: the results are available more quickly and the patient is still present. Once reliable results have been produced, they can then be interpreted to influence patient care. If the results are to be interpreted by someone *other than the patient's medical practitioner*, then guidelines for interpretation and advice should be defined in advance. These guidelines may include other factors which need to be considered, and whether other healthcare professionals are to be involved in the case of abnormal results.

- *WHO WILL SUPPLY EXPERT HELP IN INTERPRETATION ?*

You may need support in arranging further clinical advice, which may be sought from your local hospital laboratory, or in the solving of analytical problems, this may also be sought from your local hospital laboratory staff or the manufacturers of the equipment. It is likely that support will be more readily offered if the criteria for referral have been agreed in advance.

FURTHER READING

Safe working and the prevention of infection in clinical laboratories Health Services Advisory Committee. HMSO 1991.

Safe working and the prevention of infection in clinical laboratories; model rules for staff and visitors. Health Services Advisory Committee. HMSO 1991.

HN (Hazard) (87) 13. Blood glucose measurements; reliability of results produced in extra-laboratory areas.

Guidelines to Good Practice: Outstationing of Diagnostic Equipment. Appendix 6 of 'Review of pathology services staffing: A report to the manpower planning advisory group.' Management Advisory Service to the NHS.

Quality assessment of blood glucose monitors in use outside the hospital laboratory. Drucker RF, Williams DRR, Price CPJ Clin. Pathol 1983; **36**: 948-953.

Consumer Protection Act 1987. See Bulletin of the Royal College of Pathologists No. 67, June 1989, p 8-9.

Essential considerations in the provision of near-patient testing facilities. Marks V. Ann Clin Biochem. 1988; **25**: 220-225.8

Organisation and quality control of extra-laboratory blood glucose measurements. Price, CP, Burrin, JM, Nattrass, MDiab Med. 1988; **5**: 705-709.

Quality of plasma cholesterol measurements in primary care. Broughton PMG, Bullock DG, Cramb R. BMJ 1989; **298**: 297-298.

Desktop laboratory technology in General Practice Stott NCH BMJ 1989; **229**: 579-580.

The use of diagnostic equipment outside the diagnostic laboratory (1990). Evans SJ, McVittie JD, Kay JDS, Oxford Regional Health Authority.

The Control of Substances Hazardous to Health Regulations 1988 HMSO.

Guidelines on the control of Near-Patient Tests (NPT) and procedures performed on patients by non-Pathology Staff (1993). Available from D Kelshaw, Secretary, Joint Working Group on Quality Assurance c/o Mast House, Derby Road, Liverpool, L20 1EA, U.K.

HN (Hazard) (89) 31: Blood Gas Measurements: The need for reliability of results produced in extra-laboratory areas.

Index

D

E

F

G

H

I

K

L

P

Q

R

S